# COMPENDIUM OF THE CONFEDERATE ARMIES

# MISSISSIPPI

*Stewart Sifakis*

Facts On File®

AN INFOBASE HOLDINGS COMPANY

*To*
*The Memory of James Sifakis*
*1893–1961*

## COMPENDIUM OF THE CONFEDERATE ARMIES: MISSISSIPPI

Facts On File, Inc.
460 Park Avenue South
New York NY 10016

**Library of Congress Cataloging-in-Publication Data**

Sifakis, Stewart.
    Compendium of the Confederate armies / Stewart Sifakis.
       p.  cm.
    Includes bibliographical references and indexes.
    Contents: Alabama — Florida and Arkansas — [etc.]
    — Mississippi.
    ISBN 0-8160-2292-5
       1. Confederate States of America.  Army—History.
2. United States—History—Civil War, 1861–1865—Regimental histories. I.  Title.
E546.S58   1992                973.7'42            90-23631

Facts On File books are available at special discounts when purchased in bulk quantities for businesses, associations, institutions or sales promotions. Please call our Special Sales Department in New York at 212/683-2244 or 800/322-8755.

Text design by Ron Monteleone
Printed in the United States of America

MP FOF 10 9 8 7 6 5 4 3 2 1
This book is printed on acid-free paper.

# CONTENTS

# ACKNOWLEDGMENTS

I am deeply indebted for this work to the personnel, past and present, of Facts On File, especially to Edward Knappman, Gerry Helferich, and my editors: Kate Kelly, Helen Flynn, Eleanora von Dehsen, Traci Cothran, Nicholas Bakalar, Susan Schwartz and Michelle Fellner. Thanks also go to Joe Reilly, Michael Laraque, Jackie Massa and Kevin Rawlings. Also I would like to thank the staffs of the National Archives, Library of Congress, the various state archives and the New York Public Library for their patience and assistance. Over the past decades the staff of the National Park Service, Edwin C. Bearss, chief historian, have proven very informative on my frequent visits to the various battlefields. To Shaun and Christina Potter and Sally Gadsby I am indebted for keeping me at my work. For the logistical support of the management of the Hotel Post, Zermatt (Karl Ivarsson, Ursula Waeny and Lesley Dawkins), I am very grateful. And last, but certainly not least, I owe thanks to John Warren for his knowledge of computers, without which this project would have ground to a halt, and to his computer widow, Evelyne.

# INTRODUCTION

This work is intended to be the companion set to Frederick H. Dyer's *Compendium of the War of the Rebellion* for the Confederacy. The compendium was first published as a three-volume work in 1909. A study of all the Union regiments, battalions, batteries and independent companies, it has since been reprinted in two- and one-volume editions.

It has been estimated that for every day since the end of the American Civil War, one book, magazine or newspaper article has appeared dealing with some aspect of that fratricidal struggle. Many ask: If so much has been written on the Civil War, is there really a need for more? The answer is an emphatic yes. Many aspects of the conflict have been covered only superficially and require much more in-depth research. But for such research a bedrock of reference works is essential.

There are many such works available, including the U.S. War Department's 128-volume *The War of the Rebellion: A Compilation of the Official Records of the Union and Confederate Armies* and the U.S. Navy Department's 31-volume *Official Records of the Union and Confederate Navies in the War of the Rebellion*. Registers of military personnel include: George W. Cullum's two-volume *Biographical Register of the Officers and Graduates of the United States Military Academy*, Francis B. Heitman's two-volume *Historical Register and Dictionary of the United States Army From Its Organization, September 29, 1789, to March 2, 1903*, Guy V. Henry's two-volume *Military Record of Civilian Appointments in the United States Army*, Robert K. Krick's *Lee's Colonels: A Biographical Register of the Field Officers of the Army of Northern Virginia* and Ezra J. Warner's *Generals in Gray: Lives of the Confederate Commanders* and *Generals in Blue: Lives of the Union Commanders*. Politics are covered in Jon L. Wakelyn's *Biographical Dictionary of the Confederacy* and Ezra J. Warner's and W. Buck Yearns' *Biographical Register of the Confederate Congress*. E. B. Long's *The Civil War Day by Day: An Almanac 1861-1865* provides an excellent chronology. Collective biographies include Mark M. Boatner's *The Civil War Dictionary*, Patricia L. Faust's *Historical Times Illustrated Encyclopedia of the Civil War* and Stewart Sifakis' *Who Was Who in the Civil War*. Then, of course there is Dyer's compendium.

To date there has not been a comprehensive equivalent to Dyer's work for the South as a whole. Basically work has been done by individual states. North

Carolina has an excellent work currently nearing completion. Other commendable works have been done for Tennessee, Virginia and Texas. Works were begun for Georgia and South Carolina but did not proceed far. State government agencies in Florida and Kentucky made some efforts in the early years after the war. However, none of these draws a consolidated picture of the Confederate States Army. That is where the *Compendium of the Confederate Armies* comes in.

This work is organized into volumes by state. One volume includes the border state units—Kentucky, Maryland and Missouri; units organized directly by the Confederate authorities from various state companies; and those units from the Indian nations allied with the Confederacy. The final volume consists of the tables of organization of the various armies and departments throughout the war.

There are chapters in each volume on the artillery, cavalry and infantry. Those units having a numerical designation are listed first, followed by those units using the name of their commander, home region or some other name. Units are then broken down alphabetically by size—for example, battalions, batteries, companies and regiments. If two or more units still have the same sorting features, they are then further broken down alphabetically by any special designation—1st or 2nd Organization, Local Defense Troops, Militia, Provisional Army, Regulars, Reserves, Sharpshooters, State Guard, State Line, State Troops or Volunteers and so on. The company designation for artillery batteries that served within an artillery battalion or regiment is listed at the end of the battalion or regiment designation. If heavy artillery battalions or regiments served together as a unit through most of the war, they are treated as a whole with no breakdown of the companies.

Each entry starts with the unit's name. Any nicknames or other mistaken designations follow. Then comes a summary of its organizational details: its date and location of organization, mustering into service, the number of companies for battalion organizations, armament for artillery batteries, surrenders, paroles, exchanges and disbandment or mustering out. The next paragraph starts with the first commanding officer and continues with an alphabetical listing of the other field-grade officers. (Captains are listed chronologically for artillery batteries.) The next paragraph is the brigade and higher-level command assignments of the unit. This is followed by a listing of the battles and campaigns the unit was engaged in. Note that the unit was not necessarily present on each date that is indicated for multiday actions. The final paragraph is the suggested further reading, if any.

Because records are incomplete, I have dropped the list of casualties of each unit that Dyer includes for the Northern units. But I have added to Dyer's format by including the first commanding officer and the field-grade officers of each unit. Selected bibliographies are included for each volume. Also, as available, unit histories and personal memoirs are listed with some units as suggested further reading.

# MISSISSIPPI

# MISSISSIPPI UNITS

Mississippi seceded from the Union on January 9, 1861.

There were several specialized types of units organized for the army. The Confederate Congress passed an act authorizing the creation of local Defense Troops units on August 21, 1861. However the Confederate Adjutant and Inspector General's Office did not issue its General Orders #86 outlining the regulations for their organization until June 23, 1863. These units were usually organized on the company and battalion level for defense of the areas in which they were raised. They were frequently composed of employees of government arsenals, armories, bureaus, etc. or from men detailed from regular line units for detached service. Toward the end of the war some of these units were organized into regiments. These units were only to be called into active service when the situation in the vicinity required it.

The Confederate Congress created the Reserves on February 17, 1864, when it expanded conscription to include all white males between 17 and 50 years of age. Those under 18 and those over 45 were to be organized in the Reserves, troops that did not have to serve beyond the boundaries of the state.

# ARTILLERY

## 1. MISSISSIPPI 1ST ARTILLERY BATTERY

*Organization:*  Organized from the paroled prisoners of Company H, 1st Light Artillery Regiment in mid-1864.  It was armed with four guns on November 19, 1864 and served as heavy artillery in May 1865. Surrendered by General E. Kirby Smith, commanding the Trans-Mississippi Department, on May 26, 1865.

*First Commander:*  Benjamin Wade (Captain)

*Assignments:*  8th Mounted Artillery Battalion, Unattached, Trans-Mississippi Department (September-November 1864)

Reserve Artillery Battalion, Trans-Mississippi Department (November 1864)

Semmes' Horse Artillery Battalion, 2nd (Maxey's) Texas Cavalry Division, 1st Corps, Trans-Mississippi Department (December 1864-January 1865)

McMahan's Battalion Reserve Artillery, Trans-Mississippi Department (May 1865)

## 2. MISSISSIPPI 1ST LIGHT ARTILLERY REGIMENT

*Organization:*  Organized in early 1862.  Regiment surrendered at Vicksburg, Warren County, Mississippi on July 4, 1863.  Paroled at Vicksburg, Warren County, Mississippi in July 1863.  Declared exchanged on September 12, 1863. Surrendered by Lieutenant General Richard Taylor, commanding the Department of Alabama, Mississippi, and East Louisiana, at Citronelle, Alabama on May 4, 1865.  SEE:  Individual batteries following.

*First Commander:*  William T. Withers (Colonel)

*Field Officers:*  Benjamin R. Holmes (Major)

James P. Parker (Lieutenant Colonel)

Jefferson L. Wofford (Major)

## 3. MISSISSIPPI 1ST LIGHT ARTILLERY REGIMENT, COMPANY A

*Organization:*  Organized in early 1862.  Battery surrendered at Vicksburg, Warren County, Mississippi on July 4, 1863.  Paroled at Vicksburg, Warren County, Mississippi in July 1863.  Declared exchanged on September 12, 1863.  It was armed with two 6-lb. Smoothbores (brass), one 12-lb. Howitzer, and one 3.3" Rifle in May 1864.  It was armed with four guns on October 31, 1864.  Surrendered by Lieutenant General Richard Taylor, commanding the Department of Alabama, Mississippi, and East Louisiana, at Citronelle, Alabama on May 4, 1865.

*First Commander:*  Samuel J. Ridley (Captain)

*Captain:*  William T. Ratliff

*Assignments:*  Smith's Brigade, District of the Mississippi, Department #2 (June-July 1862)

2nd/3rd Sub-district, District of the Mississippi, Department #2 (July-October 1862)

Department of Mississippi and East Louisiana (October 1862)

Unattached, 2nd Military District, Department of Mississippi and East Louisiana (October 1862-January 1863)

Lee's Brigade, Smith's Division, 2nd Military District, Department of Mississippi and East Louisiana (January-February 1863)

Moore's Brigade, Forney's Division, Department of Mississippi and East Louisiana (April-July 1863)

Unattached, Forney's Division, Department of Mississippi and East Louisiana (November 1863-January 1864)

Unattached, Forney's Division, Department of Alabama, Mississippi, and East Louisiana (January 1864)

Artillery Battalion, Loring's Division, Department of Alabama, Mississippi, and East Louisiana (March-May 1864)

Artillery, Lee's Cavalry Corps, Department of Alabama, Mississippi, and East Louisiana (May 1864)

W. Adams' Cavalry Brigade, Department of Alabama, Mississippi, and East Louisiana (May 1864)

Mabry's Brigade, W. Adams' Cavalry Division, Department of Alabama, Mississippi, and East Louisiana (May-June 1864)

Artillery, W. Adams' Cavalry Division, Department of Alabama, Mississippi, and East Louisiana (July-August 1864)

Artillery, District North of the Homochitto, Department of Alabama, Mississippi, and East Louisiana (August-October 1864)

Artillery, District of Mississippi and East Louisiana (October 1864-May 1865)

*Battles:*  Vicksburg Bombardments (May 18-July 27, 1862)

Vicksburg Campaign (May-July 1863)

Vicksburg Siege (May-July 1863)

## 4.  MISSISSIPPI 1ST LIGHT ARTILLERY REGIMENT, COMPANY B

*Organization:*  Organized in early 1862. Surrendered at Port Hudson, Louisiana on July 8, 1863. Paroled in July 1863. Surrendered by Lieutenant General Richard Taylor, commanding the Department of Alabama, Mississippi, and East Louisiana, at Citronelle, Alabama on May 4, 1865.

*First Commander:*  A. J. Herod (Captain)

*Assignments:*  Smith's Brigade, Department of Southern Mississippi and East Louisiana (June 1862-July 1863)

2nd/3rd Sub-district, District of the Mississippi, Department #2 (July-September 1862)

1st Sub-district, District of the Mississippi, Department #2 (September-October 1862)

Department of Mississippi and East Louisiana (October 1862)

Unattached, 3rd Military District, Department of Mississippi and East Louisiana (October 1862-January 1863)

Beall's Brigade, 3rd Military District, Department of Mississippi and East Louisiana (January-July 1863)

Unattached, Forney's Division, Department of Mississippi and East Louisiana (November 1863-January 1864)

Unattached, Forney's Division, Department of Alabama, Mississippi, and East Louisiana (January 1864)

Artillery Brigade, District of the Gulf, Department of Alabama, Mississippi, and East Louisiana (April-June 1864)

Burnet's Command, Artillery Reserves, Defenses of Mobile, Artillery Reserves, etc., District of the Gulf, Department of Alabama, Mississippi, and East Louisiana (March-April 1865)

Burnet's Command, Department of Alabama, Mississippi, and East Louisiana (April-May 1865)

*Battles:*  Vicksburg Bombardments (May 18-July 27, 1862)

Port Hudson Bombardment (March 14, 1863)

Port Hudson Siege (May-July 1863)

Mobile (March 17-April 12, 1865)

## 5.  MISSISSIPPI 1ST LIGHT ARTILLERY REGIMENT, COMPANY C

*Organization:*  Organized in early 1862. Battery surrendered at Vicksburg, Warren County, Mississippi on July 4, 1863. Paroled at Vicksburg, Warren County, Mississippi in July 1863. Declared exchanged on September 12, 1863. Surrendered by Lieutenant General Richard Taylor, commanding the Department of Alabama, Mississippi, and East Louisiana, at Citronelle, Alabama on May 4, 1865.

**First Commander:**  H. P. Turner (Captain)

**Captain:**  L. A. Collier

**Assignments:**  Smith's Brigade, District of the Mississippi, Department #2 (June-July 1862)

2nd/3rd Sub-district, District of the Mississippi, Department #2 (July-October 1862)

Department of Mississippi and East Louisiana (October 1862)

Unattached, 2nd Military District, Department of Mississippi and East Louisiana (October 1862-January 1863)

Lee's Brigade, Smith's Division, 2nd Military District, Department of Mississippi and East Louisiana (January-February 1863)

Featherston's Brigade, Loring's Division, 2nd Military District, Department of Mississippi and East Louisiana (March-April 1863)

Moore's Brigade, Forney's Division, Department of Mississippi and East Louisiana (April-July 1863)

Unattached, Forney's Division, Department of Mississippi and East Louisiana (November 1863-January 1864)

Unattached, Forney's Division, Department of Alabama, Mississippi, and East Louisiana (January 1864)

Artillery Brigade, District of the Gulf, Department of Alabama, Mississippi, and East Louisiana (May 1864)

Burnet's Command, Defenses of Mobile, Artillery Reserves, etc., District of the Gulf, Department of Alabama, Mississippi, and East Louisiana (March-April 1865)

Burnet's Command, Department of Alabama, Mississippi, and East Louisiana (April-May 1865)

**Battles:**  Vicksburg Bombardments (May 18-July 27, 1862)

Chickasaw Bayou (December 27-29, 1862)

Steele's Bayou Expedition (March 14-27, 1863)

Rolling Fork (March 20, 1863)

Vicksburg Campaign (May-July 1863)

Vicksburg Campaign (May-July 1863)

Mobile (March 17-April 12, 1865)

## 6.   MISSISSIPPI 1ST LIGHT ARTILLERY REGIMENT, COMPANY D

**Organization:**  Organized in early 1862. It was armed with one 24-lb. Howitzer, two 12-lb. Howitzers, two 6-lb. Smoothbores, and two 3" Rifles on May 19, 1863. Battery surrendered at Vicksburg, Warren County, Mississippi on July 4, 1863. Paroled at Vicksburg, Warren County, Mississippi in July 1863. Declared exchanged on September 12, 1863. Surrendered by Lieutenant General Richard Taylor, commanding the Department of Alabama, Mississippi, and East Louisiana, at Citronelle, Alabama on May 4, 1865.

*First Commander:* Jefferson L. Wofford (Captain)

*Assignments:* Smith's Brigade, District of the Mississippi, Department #2 (June-July 1862)

2nd/3rd Sub-district, District of the Mississippi, Department #2 (July-October 1862)

Department of Mississippi and East Louisiana (October 1862)

Unattached, 2nd Military District, Department of Mississippi and East Louisiana (October-December 1862)

Thomas' Brigade, Lee's-Maury's Provisional Division, 2nd Military District, Department of Mississippi and East Louisiana (December 1862-January 1863)

Lee's-Moore's Brigade, Smith's Division, 2nd Military District, Department of Mississippi and East Louisiana (January-April 1863)

Moore's Brigade, Forney's Division, Department of Mississippi and East Louisiana (April-July 1863)

Unattached, Forney's Division, Department of Mississippi and East Louisiana (November 1863-January 1864)

Unattached, Forney's Division, Department of Alabama, Mississippi, and East Louisiana (January 1864)

Artillery Brigade, District of the Gulf, Department of Alabama, Mississippi, and East Louisiana (May 1864)

Burnet's Command, Defenses of Mobile, Artillery Reserves, etc., District of the Gulf, Department of Alabama, Mississippi, and East Louisiana (March-April 1865)

Burnet's Command, Department of Alabama, Mississippi, and East Louisiana (April-May 1865)

*Battles:* Vicksburg Bombardments (May 18-July 27, 1862)

Vicksburg Campaign (May-July 1863)

Vicksburg Campaign (May-July 1863)

Mobile (March 17-April 12, 1865)

## 7. MISSISSIPPI 1ST LIGHT ARTILLERY REGIMENT, COMPANY E

*Organization:* Organized in early 1862. Battery surrendered at Vicksburg, Warren County, Mississippi on July 4, 1863. Paroled at Vicksburg, Warren County, Mississippi in July 1863. It was apparently never reorganized.

*First Commander:* Newit J. Drew (Captain)

*Assignments:* Smith's Brigade, District of the Mississippi, Department #2 (June-July 1862)

2nd/3rd Sub-district, District of the Mississippi, Department #2 (July-October 1862)

Department of Mississippi and East Louisiana (October 1862)

Unattached, 2nd Military District, Department of Mississippi and East Louisiana (October-December 1862)

Thomas' Brigade, Lee's-Maury's Provisional Division, 2nd Military District, Department of Mississippi and East Louisiana (December 1862-January 1863)

Lee's-Moore's Brigade, Smith's Division, 2nd Military District, Department of Mississippi and East Louisiana (January-April 1863)

Moore's Brigade, Forney's Division, Department of Mississippi and East Louisiana (April-July 1863)

**Battles:** Vicksburg Bombardments (May 18-July 27, 1862)

Chickasaw Bayou (December 27-29, 1862)

Vicksburg Campaign (May-July 1863)

Vicksburg Siege (May-July 1863)

## 8.   MISSISSIPPI 1ST LIGHT ARTILLERY REGIMENT, COMPANY F

*Organization:*   Organized in early 1862.   Surrendered at Port Hudson, Louisiana on July 8, 1863.   Paroled in late 1864.   Reorganized with the guns of Barlow's (Louisiana) Artillery Battery in October 1864. It was armed with two 3.67" Sawyers and two 9-lb. Napoleons in October 1864. Surrendered by Lieutenant General Richard Taylor, commanding the Department of Alabama, Mississippi, and East Louisiana, at Citronelle, Alabama on May 4, 1865.

*First Commander:*   J. L. Bradford (Captain)

*Assignments:*   Smith's Brigade, District of the Mississippi, Department #2 (June-July 1862)

2nd/3rd Sub-district, District of the Mississippi, Department #2 (July-October 1862)

Department of Mississippi and East Louisiana (October 1862)

Unattached, 2nd Military District, Department of Mississippi and East Louisiana (October 1862-January 1863)

Beall's Brigade, 3rd Military District, Department of Mississippi and East Louisiana (January-July 1863)

District South of Homochitto, Department of Alabama, Mississippi, and East Louisiana (October 1864)

Artillery, [Sub-]district of Southwest Mississippi and East Louisiana, District of Mississippi and East Louisiana, Department of Alabama, Mississippi, and East Louisiana (October 1864-May 1865)

**Battles:** Vicksburg Bombardments (May 18-July 27, 1862)

Port Hudson Bombardment (March 14, 1863)

Port Hudson Siege (May-July 1863)

## 9. MISSISSIPPI 1ST LIGHT ARTILLERY REGIMENT, COMPANY G

**Organization:** Organized in early 1862. Regiment surrendered at Vicksburg, Warren County, Mississippi on July 4, 1863. Paroled at Vicksburg, Warren County, Mississippi in July 1863. Declared exchanged on September 12, 1863. It was armed with four 12-lb. Napoleons on May 1, 1864. Surrendered by Lieutenant General Richard Taylor, commanding the Department of Alabama, Mississippi, and East Louisiana, at Citronelle, Alabama on May 4, 1865.

**First Commander:** James J. Cowan (Captain)

**Assignments:** Smith's Brigade, District of the Mississippi, Department #2 (June-July 1862)

2nd/3rd Military District, District of the Mississippi, Department #2 (July-October 1862)

Department of Mississippi and East Louisiana (October 1862)

Unattached, 2nd Military District, Department of Mississippi and East Louisiana (October 1862-January 1863)

Hébert's Brigade, Maury's Division, 2nd Military District, Department of Mississippi and East Louisiana (January-February 1863)

Tilghman's Brigade, Loring's Division, Department of Mississippi and East Louisiana (April-May 1863)

Unattached, Forney's Division, Department of Mississippi and East Louisiana (November 1863-January 1864)

Unattached, Forney's Division, Department of Alabama, Mississippi, and East Louisiana (January 1864)

Artillery Battalion, Loring's Division, Department of Alabama, Mississippi, and East Louisiana (March-May 1864)

Artillery Battalion, Loring's Division, Army of Mississippi (May-July 1864)

Myrick's Battalion, Artillery, 3rd Corps, Army of Tennessee (July 1864-January 1865)

Grayson's Artillery Battalion, Right Wing, Defenses of Mobile, Artillery Reserves, etc., District of the Gulf, Department of Alabama, Mississippi, and East Louisiana (March-April 1865)

Grayson's Battalion, Smith's Artillery Regiment, Department of Alabama, Mississippi, and East Louisiana (April-May 1865)

**Battles:** Vicksburg Bombardments (May 18-July 27, 1862)

Vicksburg Campaign (May-July 1863)

Vicksburg Siege (May-July 1863)

Atlanta Campaign (May-September 1864)

Atlanta Siege (July-September 1864)

Nashville (December 15-16, 1864)

Mobile (March 17-April 12, 1865)

## 10.  MISSISSIPPI 1ST LIGHT ARTILLERY REGIMENT, COMPANY H

*Nickname:*  Connor Battery

*Organization:*  Organized at Natchez on April 30, 1862.  It was armed with two 6-lb. Smoothbores and two 12-lb. Howitzers at its organization.  Battery surrendered at Vicksburg, Warren County, Mississippi on July 4, 1863.  Paroled at Vicksburg, Warren County, Mississippi in July 1863. Declared exchanged on September 12, 1863.  Reorganized and designated as the 1st Mississippi Battery.

*First Commander:*  George Ralston (Captain)

*Captain:*  Benjamin Wade

*Assignments:*  Port Hudson, Department #1 (April-June 1862)

Smith's Brigade, Department of Southern Mississippi and East Louisiana (June-July 1862)

1st Sub-district, District of the Mississippi, Department #2 (July-September 1862)

Department of Mississippi and East Louisiana (October 1862)

Unattached, 3rd Military District, Department of Mississippi and East Louisiana (October-December 1862)

Hébert's Brigade, Maury's Division, 2nd Military District, Department of Mississippi and East Louisiana (December 1862-February 1863)

Moore's Brigade, Maury's-Forney's Division, Department of Mississippi and East Louisiana (April-July 1863)

*Battles:*  Vicksburg Bombardments (May 18-July 27, 1862)

Georgia Landing, near Labadieville (October 27, 1862)

Chickasaw Bayou (December 27-29, 1862)

Vicksburg Campaign (May-July 1863)

Vicksburg Siege (May-July 1863)

## 11.  MISSISSIPPI 1ST LIGHT ARTILLERY REGIMENT, COMPANY I

*Organization:*  Organized in the spring of 1862.  Battery surrendered at Vicksburg, Warren County, Mississippi on July 4, 1863.  Paroled at Vicksburg, Warren County, Mississippi in July 1863.  Declared exchanged on September 12, 1863.  Surrendered by Lieutenant General Richard Taylor, commanding the Department of Alabama, Mississippi, and East Louisiana, at Citronelle, Alabama on May 4, 1865.

*First Commander:*  Robert Bowman (Captain)

*Assignments:*  Smith's Brigade, District of the Mississippi, Department #2 (June-July 1862)

2nd/3rd Sub-district, District of the Mississippi, Department #2 (July-October 1862)

Department of Mississippi and East Louisiana (October 1862)

Unattached, 2nd Military District, Department of Mississippi and East Louisiana (October-December 1862)

Thomas' Brigade, Lee's-Maury's Provisional Division, 2nd Military District, Department of Mississippi and East Louisiana (December 1862-January 1863)

Lee's Brigade, Smith's Division, 2nd Military District, Department of Mississippi and East Louisiana (January-February 1863)

Vaughn's Brigade, Smith's Division, 2nd Military District, Department of Mississippi and East Louisiana (March-April 1863)

Moore's Brigade, Forney's Division, Department of Mississippi and East Louisiana (April-July 1863)

Unattached, Forney's Division, Department of Mississippi and East Louisiana (November 1863-January 1864)

Unattached, Forney's Division, Department of Alabama, Mississippi, and East Louisiana (January 1864)

Artillery Brigade, District of the Gulf, Department of Alabama, Mississippi, and East Louisiana (April 1864)

Burnet's Command, Right Wing, Defenses of Mobile, Artillery Reserves, etc., District of the Gulf, Department of Alabama, Mississippi, and East Louisiana (March-April 1865)

Burnet's Command, Department of Alabama, Mississippi, and East Louisiana (April-May 1865)

**Battles:** Vicksburg Bombardments (May 18-July 27, 1862)

Chickasaw Bayou (December 27-29, 1862)

Vicksburg Campaign (May-July 1863)

Vicksburg Siege (May-July 1863)

Mobile (March 17-April 12, 1865)

## 12. MISSISSIPPI 1ST LIGHT ARTILLERY REGIMENT, COMPANY K

*Organization:*  Organized in the spring of 1862. Surrendered at Port Hudson, Louisiana on July 8, 1863. Paroled in July 1863. It was armed with four 12-lb. Napoleons from October 31, 1864 to February 25, 1865. Surrendered by Lieutenant General Richard Taylor, commanding the Department of Alabama, Mississippi, and East Louisiana, at Citronelle, Alabama on May 4, 1865.

*First Commander:*  George F. Abbay (Captain)

*Assignments:*  Smith's Brigade, Department of Southern Mississippi and East Louisiana (June-July 1862)

2nd/3rd Sub-district, District of the Mississippi, Department #2 (July-September 1862)

1st Sub-district, District of the Mississippi, Department #2 (September-October 1862)

Department of Mississippi and East Louisiana (October 1862)

Unattached, 3rd Military District, Department of Mississippi and East Louisiana (October 1862-January 1863)

Beall's Brigade, 3rd Military District, Department of Mississippi and East Louisiana (January-July 1863)

Unattached, Forney's Division, Department of Mississippi and East Louisiana (November 1863-January 1864)

Unattached, Forney's Division, Department of Alabama, Mississippi, and East Louisiana (January 1864)

Artillery Brigade, District of the Gulf, Department of Alabama, Mississippi, and East Louisiana (May-July 1864)

Thomas' Brigade, District of the Gulf, Department of Alabama, Mississippi, and East Louisiana (September-October 1864)

Burnet's Command, District of the Gulf, Department of Alabama, Mississippi, and East Louisiana (October-November 1864)

Artillery, District of the Gulf, Department of Alabama, Mississippi, and East Louisiana (November 1864)

Semple's Artillery Battalion, District of the Gulf, Department of Alabama, Mississippi, and East Louisiana (November 1864-February 1865)

Cockrell's Brigade, French's Division, District of the Gulf, Department of Alabama, Mississippi, and East Louisiana (March-April 1865)

Cockrell's Brigade, French's Division, Department of Alabama, Mississippi, and East Louisiana (April-May 1865)

**Battles:** Vicksburg Bombardments (May 18-July 27, 1862)

Port Hudson Bombardment (March 14, 1863)

Port Hudson Siege (May-July 1863)

Mobile (March 17-April 12, 1865)


### 13. MISSISSIPPI 1ST LIGHT ARTILLERY REGIMENT, COMPANY L

*Also Known As:* Vaiden Artillery

*Organization:* Organized in the spring of 1862. Battery surrendered at Vicksburg, Warren County, Mississippi on July 4, 1863. Paroled at Vicksburg, Warren County, Mississippi in July 1863. Declared exchanged on September 12, 1863. Surrendered by Lieutenant General Richard Taylor, commanding the Department of Alabama, Mississippi, and East Louisiana, at Citronelle, Alabama on May 4, 1865.

*First Commander:* Samuel C. Bains (Captain)

*Assignments:* Smith's Brigade, District of the Mississippi, Department #2 (June-July 1862)

2nd/3rd Sub-district, District of the Mississippi, Department #2 (July-October 1862)

Department of Mississippi and East Louisiana (October 1862)

Unattached, 2nd Military District, Department of Mississippi and East Louisiana (October 1862-January 1863)

Beltzhoover's Brigade, Smith's Division, 2nd Military District, Department of Mississippi and East Louisiana (January-February 1863)

Lee's Brigade, Smith's Division, 2nd Military District, Department of Mississippi and East Louisiana (March-April 1863)

River Batteries, Vicksburg, Department of Mississippi and East Louisiana (April-July 1863)

Heavy Artillery Brigade, Forney's Command, Department of Mississippi and East Louisiana (November 1863-January 1864)

Burnet's Command, Defenses of Mobile, Artillery Reserves, etc., District of the Gulf, Department of Alabama, Mississippi, and East Louisiana (March-April 1865)

Burnet's Command, Department of Alabama, Mississippi, and East Louisiana (April-May 1865)

*Battles:* Vicksburg Bombardments (May 18-July 27, 1862)

Vicksburg Passage (April 16, 1863)

Vicksburg Campaign (May-July 1863)

Vicksburg Siege (May-July 1863)

Mobile (March 17-April 12, 1865)

## 14.  MISSISSIPPI 11TH HEAVY ARTILLERY BATTALION

*See:* TENNESSEE 1ST HEAVY ARTILLERY BATTALION

## 15.  MISSISSIPPI 14TH LIGHT ARTILLERY BATTALION

*Organization:* Organized with three companies in the spring of 1862. Battalion surrendered at Vicksburg, Warren County, Mississippi on July 4, 1863. Paroled at Vicksburg, Warren County, Mississippi in July 1863. Declared exchanged on September 12, 1863. Disappears from the records in January 1864. SEE: Individual batteries following.

*First Commander:* Matthew S. Ward (Major)

## 16.  MISSISSIPPI 14TH LIGHT ARTILLERY BATTALION, COMPANY A

*Organization:* Organized in the spring of 1862. Battery surrendered at Vicksburg, Warren County, Mississippi on July 4, 1863. Paroled at Vicksburg,

Warren County, Mississippi in July 1863. Declared exchanged on September 12, 1863. Disappears from the records in January 1864.

**First Commander:** J. D. Vance (Captain)

**Assignments:** Grenada, Mississippi, Department #2 (June 1862)

2nd/3rd Sub-district, District of the Mississippi, Department #2 (July-October 1862)

Department of Mississippi and East Louisiana (October 1862)

2nd Military District, Department of Mississippi and East Louisiana (October-December 1862)

Thomas' Brigade, Lee's-Maury's Provisional Division, 2nd Military District, Department of Mississippi and East Louisiana (December 1862-January 1863)

Unattached, Smith's Division, 2nd Military District, Department of Mississippi and East Louisiana (January 1863)

Vaughn's Brigade, Smith's Division, 2nd Military District, Department of Mississippi and East Louisiana (April 1863)

Vaughn's Brigade, Smith's Division, Department of Mississippi and East Louisiana (April 1863)

Unattached, Smith's Division, Department of Mississippi and East Louisiana (April-July 1863)

Baldwin's Brigade, Forney's Division, Department of Mississippi and East Louisiana (November 1863)

Beltzhoover's Brigade, Forney's Division, Department of Mississippi and East Louisiana (November 1863-January 1864)

**Battles:** Chickasaw Bayou (December 27-29, 1862)

Vicksburg Passage (April 16, 1863)

Vicksburg Campaign (May-July 1863)

Vicksburg Siege (May-July 1863)

## 17.   MISSISSIPPI 14TH LIGHT ARTILLERY BATTALION, COMPANY B

**Organization:** Organized in the spring of 1862. Battery surrendered at Vicksburg, Warren County, Mississippi on July 4, 1863. Paroled at Vicksburg, Warren County, Mississippi in July 1863. Declared exchanged on September 12, 1863. It was armed with four 12-lb. Napoleons on May 24, 1864. Disappears from the records in September 1864.

**First Commander:** James H. Yates (Captain)

**Assignments:** Grenada, Mississippi, Department #2 (June 1862)

3rd/2nd Sub-district, District of the Mississippi, Department #2 (July-October 1862)

Department of Mississippi and East Louisiana (October 1862)

2nd Military District, Department of Mississippi and East Louisiana (October-December 1862)

Thomas' Brigade, Lee's-Maury's Provisional Division, 2nd Military District, Department of Mississippi and East Louisiana (December 1862-January 1863)

Unattached, Smith's Division, 2nd Military District, Department of Mississippi and East Louisiana (January 1863)

Vaughn's Brigade, Smith's Division, 2nd Military District, Department of Mississippi and East Louisiana (April 1863)

Vaughn's Brigade, Smith's Division, Department of Mississippi and East Louisiana (April 1863)

Unattached, Smith's Division, Department of Mississippi and East Louisiana (April-July 1863)

Baldwin's Brigade, Forney's Division, Department of Mississippi and East Louisiana (November 1863)

Beltzhoover's Brigade, Forney's Division, Department of Mississippi and East Louisiana (November 1863-January 1864)

Truehart's Artillery Battalion, District of the Gulf, Department of Alabama, Mississippi, and East Louisiana (May 1864)

Artillery Battalion, Cantey's-Walthall's Division, Army of Mississippi (June-July 1864)

Preston's-Truehart's Battalion, Artillery, Army of Mississippi (July 1864)

Truehart's Battalion, Artillery, 3rd Corps, Army of Tennessee (July-September 1864)

**Battles:**  Chickasaw Bayou (December 27-29, 1862)

Vicksburg Passage (April 16, 1863)

Vicksburg Campaign (May-July 1863)

Vicksburg Siege (May-July 1863)

Atlanta Campaign (May-September 1864)

Atlanta Siege (July-September 1864)

## 18.  MISSISSIPPI 14TH LIGHT ARTILLERY BATTALION, COMPANY C

**Organization:**  Organized in the spring of 1862. It was armed with four guns in July 1863. It was armed with two 6-lb. Smoothbores on January 5, 1864. Surrendered by Lieutenant General Richard Taylor, commanding the Department of Alabama, Mississippi, and East Louisiana, at Meridian, Mississippi on May 4, 1865.

**First Commander:**  J. M. McLendon (Captain)

**Captain:**  F. W. Merrin

**Assignments:**  Grenada, Mississippi, Department #2 (June 1862)

3rd/2nd Sub-district, District of the Mississippi, Department #2 (July-October 1862)

Department of Mississippi and East Louisiana (October 1862)

2nd Military District, Department of Mississippi and East Louisiana (October-December 1862)

Thomas' Brigade, Lee's-Maury's Provisional Division, 2nd Military District, Department of Mississippi and East Louisiana (December 1862-January 1863)

Unattached, Smith's Division, 2nd Military District, Department of Mississippi and East Louisiana (January-April 1863)

Unattached, Smith's Division, Department of Mississippi and East Louisiana (April-May 1863)

Featherston's Brigade, Loring's Division, Department of the West (May-July 1863)

Featherston's Brigade, Loring's Division, Department of Mississippi and East Louisiana (July-August 1863)

Chalmers' Cavalry Brigade, Department of Mississippi and East Louisiana (September-October 1863)

Slemons' Brigade, Chalmers' Cavalry Division, Department of Mississippi and East Louisiana (October 1863-November 1864)

Slemons' Brigade, Chalmers' Division, Lee's Cavalry Corps, Department of Mississippi and East Louisiana (November 1863-January 1864)

Slemons' Brigade, Chalmers' Division, Lee's Cavalry Corps, Department of Mississippi and East Louisiana (January-March 1864)

Slemons' Brigade, Chalmers' Division, Forrest's Cavalry Corps, Department of Alabama, Mississippi, and East Louisiana (March-June 1864)

Artillery, District of Central Alabama, Department of Alabama, Mississippi, and East Louisiana (October 1864-May 1865)

**Battles:** Chickasaw Bayou (December 27-29, 1862)

Vicksburg Passage (April 16, 1863)

Vicksburg Campaign (May-July 1863)

Jackson Siege (July 1863)

Chalmers' Raid in West Tennessee and North Mississippi [detachment] (October 4-17, 1863)

## 19.   MISSISSIPPI BROOKHAVEN LIGHT ARTILLERY BATTERY

**Organization:**   Organized in early 1862. It was armed with four guns on May 14, 1863. It was armed with two 6-lb. Smoothbores and two 3" Rifles on November 28, 1863. It was armed with two 6-lb. Smoothbores and two 12-lb. Howitzers on January 5, 1864. It was armed with two 3" Rifles, one 10-lb. Parrott, and one 6-lb. Smoothbore on May 1, 1864. It was armed with two

10-lb. Parrotts and two 12-lb. Napoleons on May 19, 1864. Apparently disbanded in January 1865.

**First Commander:** James A. Hoskins (Captain)

**Assignments:** Port Hudson, Department #1 (April-June 1862)

Port Hudson, Department of Southern Mississippi and East Louisiana (June-July 1862)

1st Sub-district, District of the Mississippi, Department #2 (July-October 1862)

Department of Mississippi and East Louisiana (October 1862)

3rd Military District, Department of Mississippi and East Louisiana (October 1862)

Gregg's Brigade, 3rd Military District, Department of Mississippi and East Louisiana (December 1862-May 1863)

Gist's Brigade, Department of the West (May 1863)

Adams' Brigade, Walker's Division, Department of the West (June 1863)

Ector's Brigade, French's Division, Department of Mississippi and East Louisiana (January 1864)

Ector's Brigade, French's Division, Department of Alabama, Mississippi, and East Louisiana (February 1864)

Artillery, French's Division, Department of Alabama, Mississippi, and East Louisiana (March-May 1864)

Storrs' Artillery Battalion, French's Division, Army of Mississippi (May-July 1864)

Storrs' Battalion, Artillery, Army of Mississippi (July 1864)

Storrs' Battalion, Artillery, 3rd Corps, Army of Tennessee (July 1864-January 1865)

**Battles:** Vicksburg Campaign (May-July 1863)

Jackson (May 14, 1863)

Yazoo River (May 24-31, 1863)

Atlanta Campaign (May-September 1864)

Atlanta Siege (July-September 1864)

Nashville (December 15-16, 1864)

## 20. MISSISSIPPI BUCKNER ARTILLERY BATTERY

**Organization:** Organized in the spring of 1863. It was armed with four 2-lb. Smoothbores in October 1863. It was armed with four 10 oz. Smoothbores and one 2.9" Rifle on November 28, 1863. It was armed with four 1.5625" Williams Breechloaders on January 5, 1864. No record after March 10, 1864.

**First Commander:** H. C. Holt (Lieutenant)

**Assignments:** 1st Military District, Department of Mississippi and East Louisiana (May-July 1863)

Artillery, 5th Military District, Department of Mississippi and East Louisiana (July-September 1863)

Chalmers' Cavalry Brigade, Department of Mississippi and East Louisiana (September-October 1863)

McCulloch's Brigade, Chalmers' Division, Lee's Cavalry Corps, Department of Mississippi and East Louisiana (October 1863-January 1864)

McCulloch's Brigade, Chalmers's Division, Lee's Cavalry Corps, Department of Alabama, Mississippi, and East Louisiana (January-March 1864)

**Battles:**  Operations along the Memphis and Charleston Railroad (May 19-July 4, 1863)

Chalmers' Raid in West Tennessee and North Mississippi (October 4-17, 1863)

Meridian Campaign (February-March 1864)

### 21.  MISSISSIPPI BYRNE'S ARTILLERY BATTERY

*See:* KENTUCKY BYRNE'S ARTILLERY BATTERY

### 22.  MISSISSIPPI CONFEDERATE GUARDS ARTILLERY BATTALION

**Organization:**  Organized in early 1862.  It was armed with three 20-lb. Parrotts and two 12-lb. Smoothbores on December 26, 1864.  Surrendered at Appomattox Court House, Virginia on April 9, 1865.

**First Commander:**  John C. Grisham (Captain)

**Captain:**  William D. Bradford

**Assignments:**  French's Brigade, District of the Pamlico, Department of North Carolina (March-April 1862)

Ransom's Brigade, Department of North Carolina (April 1862)

Ransom's Brigade, Department of North Carolina and Southern Virginia (August-December 1862)

Artillery, French's Command, Department of North Carolina and Southern Virginia (February-March 1863)

Artillery, Pickett's Division, Department of North Carolina and Southern Virginia (March 1863)

Artillery, Department of Southern Virginia (April-May 1863)

Artillery, French's Command, Department of North Carolina (May 1863)

Artillery, Department of North Carolina (May-June 1863)

Branch's Battalion, Artillery, Department of North Carolina (June-July 1863)

Branch's Artillery Battalion, Ransom's Division, Department of Richmond (July-September 1863)

Coit's Battalion, Artillery, Department of North Carolina and Southern Virginia (May-June 1864)

Artillery Battalion, Johnson's Division, Department of North Carolina and Southern Virginia (June 1864-June 1863)

1st Military District, Department of North Carolina and Southern Virginia [section] (June 1864)

Branch's-Coit's Battalion, Artillery, Department of North Carolina and Southern Virginia (June-October 1864)

Coit's Battalion, Artillery, 4th Corps, Army of Northern Virginia (October 1864-April 1865)

**Battles:** Suffolk Campaign (April-May 1863)

Petersburg Siege (June 1864-April 1865)

Appomattox Court House (April 9, 1865)

**Further Reading:** Hoy, Patrick Crawford, *A Brief History of Bradford's Battery.*

## 23. MISSISSIPPI CONNOR ARTILLERY BATTERY

*See:* MISSISSIPPI 1ST LIGHT ARTILLERY REGIMENT, COMPANY H

## 24. MISSISSIPPI ENGLISH'S ARTILLERY BATTERY

*See:* MISSISSIPPI QUITMAN ARTILLERY BATTERY

## 25. MISSISSIPPI GRAVES' ARTILLERY BATTERY

*See:* KENTUCKY ISSAQUENA ARTILLERY BATTERY

## 26. MISSISSIPPI INGRAMS' ARTILLERY BATTERY

*See:* KENTUCKY ISSAQUENA ARTILLERY BATTERY

## 27. MISSISSIPPI ISSAQUENA ARTILLERY BATTERY

*See:* KENTUCKY ISSAQUENA ARTILLERY BATTERY

## 28. MISSISSIPPI JEFFERSON FLYING ARTILLERY BATTERY

**Organization:** Organized at Fayette on April 3, 1861. Mustered into Confederate service at Fayette on April 3, 1861. It was armed with two 6-lb. Smoothbores and two 12-lb. Howitzers on April 6-7, 1862. It was armed with four 12-lb. Napoleons from December 14, 1863 to April 1, 1864. Apparently disbanded in December 1864.

**First Commander:** William L. Harper (Captain)

**Captain:** Putnam Darden

**Assignments:** Reserve, Central Army of Kentucky, Department #2 (October 1861-February 1862)

Wood's Brigade, Pillow's Division, Central Army of Kentucky, Department #2 (February-March 1862)

Wood's Brigade, 3rd Corps, Army of the Mississippi, Department #2 (March-May 1862)

Johnson's Brigade, Buckner's Division, Left Wing, Army of the Mississippi, Department #2 (October-November 1862)

Johnson's Brigade, Buckner's-Cleburne's Division, 2nd Corps, Army of Tennessee (November 1862-May 1863)

Johnson's Brigade, Stewart's Division, 2nd Corps, Army of Tennessee (May-September 1863)

Reserve Artillery, Buckner's Corps, Army of Tennessee (September-October 1863)

Artillery Battalion, Stewart's Division, 2nd Corps, Army of Tennessee (October-November 1863)

Williams' Battalion, Buckaler's Division, Hardee's Corp, Army of Tennessee (November 1863)

Williams' Battalion, Reserve Artillery, Army of Tennessee (November 1863-July 1864)

Williams' Battalion, Artillery, 2nd Corps, Army of Tennessee (July-September 1864)

Williams' Artillery Battalion, Macon, Georgia, Department of Tennessee (September 1864)

Myrick's Battalion, Artillery, 3rd Corps, Army of Tennessee (December 1864)

**Battles:** Shiloh (April 6-7, 1862)

Corinth Campaign (April-June 1862)

Perryville (October 8, 1862)

Murfreesboro (December 31, 1862-January 3, 1863)

Tullahoma Campaign (June 1863)

Hoover's Gap (June 24, 1863)

Chickamauga (September 19-20, 1863)

Chattanooga Siege (September-November 1863)

Chattanooga (November 23-25, 1863)

Atlanta Campaign (May-September 1864)

New Hope Church (May 25-June 4, 1864)

Atlanta Siege (July-September 1864)

Nashville (December 15-16, 1864)

## 29. MISSISSIPPI KERR'S ARTILLERY BATTERY
*See:* MISSISSIPPI QUITMAN LIGHT ARTILLERY BATTERY

## 30. MISSISSIPPI LOVELL'S ARTILLERY BATTERY
*See:* MISSISSIPPI QUITMAN ARTILLERY BATTERY

## 31. MISSISSIPPI MADISON LIGHT ARTILLERY BATTERY

*Organization:* Organized in early 1863. It was armed with three 12-lb. Napoleons and one 12-lb. Howitzer on July 1-3, 1863. It was armed with four 12-lb. Napoleons from April 9, to December 28, 1864. Also manning two 8" Mortars on December 30, 1864. Surrendered at Appomattox Court House, Virginia on April 9, 1865.

*First Commander:* George Ward (Captain)

*Captain:* Thomas J. Richards

*Assignments:* Artillery, Department of Southern Virginia (April-May 1863)

Poague's Artillery Battalion, Pender's Division, 3rd Corps, Army of Northern Virginia (May-July 1863)

Poague's Battalion, Artillery, 3rd Corps, Army of Northern Virginia (July 1863-April 1865)

*Battles:* Gettysburg (July 1-3, 1863)

Bristoe Campaign (October 1863)

Mine Run Campaign (November-December 1863)

The Wilderness (May 5-6, 1864)

Spotsylvania Court House (May 8-21, 1864)

North Anna (May 23-26, 1864)

Cold Harbor (June 1-3, 1864)

Petersburg Siege (June 1864-April 1865)

Appomattox Court House (April 9, 1865)

## 32. MISSISSIPPI PETTUS FLYING ARTILLERY BATTERY

*Organization:* Organized in the summer of 1861. It was armed with two 6-lb. Smoothbores, two 12-lb. Howitzers, and two 3" Rifles on April 6-7, 1862. It was armed with four guns on April 29, 1863. Battery surrendered at Vicksburg, Warren County, Mississippi on July 4, 1863. Paroled at Vicksburg, Warren County, Mississippi in July 1863. Declared exchanged on September 12, 1863. It was armed with two 10 lb. Parrotts and two 12-lb. Howitzers in May 1864. Surrendered by Lieutenant General Richard Taylor, commanding the Department of Alabama, Mississippi, and East Louisiana, at Meridian, Mississippi on May 4, 1865.

*First Commander:* Alfred Hudson (Captain)

*Captain:* James L. Hoole

*Assignments:* Cheatham's Brigade, 1st Geographical Division, Department #2 (September-October 1861)

Bowen's Brigade, 1st Geographical Division, Department #2 (October 1861)

Smith's Brigade, Cheatham's Division, 1st Geographical Division, Department #2 (October 1861)

2nd Brigade, Bowen's Division, 1st Geographical Division, Department #2 (November-December 1861)

Bowen's Brigade, Central Army of Kentucky, Department #2 (January-February 1862)

Bowen's Brigade, Crittenden's Division, Central Army of Kentucky, Department #2 (February-March 1862)

Bowen's Brigade, Reserve Corps, Army of the Mississippi, Department #2 (March-June 1862)

Helm's Brigade, District of the Mississippi, Department #2 (June-August 1862)

Helm's Brigade, Clark's Division, Breckinridge's Command, District of the Mississippi, Department #2 (August 1862)

Rust's Brigade, Lovell's Division, District of the Mississippi, Army of West Tennessee, Department #2 (September-October 1862)

Rust's Brigade, Lovell's Division, Lovell's Corps, Army of West Tennessee, Department of Mississippi and East Louisiana (October 1862)

Rust's Brigade, Loring's Division, Army of the Department of Mississippi and East Louisiana (January 1863)

Rust's Brigade, Loring's Division, Department of Mississippi and East Louisiana (January-March 1863)

Rust's Brigade, 3rd Military District, Department of Mississippi and East Louisiana (March-April 1863)

4th Military District, Department of Mississippi and East Louisiana (April 1863)

Attached Troops, Bowen's Division, Department of Mississippi and East Louisiana (April-May 1863)

Barton's Brigade, Stevenson's Division, Department of Mississippi and East Louisiana (May-July 1863)

Baldwin's Brigade, Forney's Division, Department of Mississippi and East Louisiana (November 1863)

Ross' Command, Forney's Division, Department of Mississippi and East Louisiana (November-December 1863)

Artillery, French's Division, Department of Alabama, Mississippi, and East Louisiana (April-May 1864)

Artillery, Forrest's Cavalry Corps, Department of Alabama, Mississippi, and East Louisiana (May-June 1864)

Unattached, Chalmers' Division, Forrest's Cavalry Corps, Department of Alabama, Mississippi, and East Louisiana (June 1864)

McCulloch's Brigade, Chalmers' Division, Forrest's Cavalry Corps, Department of Alabama, Mississippi, and East Louisiana (June-July 1864)

Artillery, Forrest's Cavalry Corps, Department of Alabama, Mississippi, and East Louisiana (July 1864-May 1865)

**Battles:** Shiloh (April 6-7, 1862)
Corinth Campaign (April-June 1862)
Vicksburg Bombardments (May 18-July 27, 1862)
Baton Rouge (August 5, 1862)
Corinth (October 3-4, 1862)
Grand Gulf (April 29, 1863)
Vicksburg Campaign (May-July 1863)
Port Gibson (May 1, 1863)
Vicksburg Siege (May-July 1863)
Forrest's Raid into Northern Alabama and Middle Tennessee [section] (September 16-October 10, 1864)
Athens (September 24, 1864)
Tupelo (July 14, 1864)
Forrest's West Tennessee Raid (December 11, 1862-January 3, 1863)
Wilson's Raid (March-April 1865)

## 33. MISSISSIPPI QUITMAN ARTILLERY BATTERY

**Organization:** Organized at Natchez in late 1861. It had no guns on April 30, 1862. Surrendered at Port Hudson, Louisiana on July 8, 1863. Paroled in July 1863. Apparently never reorganized.
**First Commander:** William S. Lovell (Captain)
**Captain:** R. T. English
**Assignments:** Port Hudson, Department #1 (April-May 1862)
Department of Southern Mississippi and East Louisiana (June-July 1862)
2nd Sub-district, District of the Mississippi, Department #2 (July-August 1862)
Artillery, 1st Sub-district, District of the Mississippi, Department #2 (August-October 1862)
Artillery, 1st Sub-district, Department of Mississippi and East Louisiana (October 1862)
Artillery, 3rd Military District, Department of Mississippi and East Louisiana (October 1862-April 1863)
Provost Guard, 3rd Military District, Department of Mississippi and East Louisiana (April-May 1863)
3rd Military District, Department of Mississippi and East Louisiana (May-July 1863)
**Battle:** Port Hudson Siege (May-July 1863)

## 34. MISSISSIPPI QUITMAN LIGHT ARTILLERY BATTERY

**Organization:** Organized in 1861. It was armed with three guns from May to July 1863. Apparently disbanded in 1863.
**First Commander:** J. F. Kerr (Captain)

*Assignments:*  District of the Mississippi, Department #2 (May-July 1862)
Artillery, 5th Military District, Department of Mississippi and East Louisiana (May-July 1863)
*Battles:*  Vicksburg Bombardments (May 18-July 27, 1862)
Operations along the Memphis and Charleston Railroad (May 19-July 4, 1863)

### 35.  MISSISSIPPI ROBERTS' ARTILLERY BATTERY
*See:* MISSISSIPPI SEVEN STARS ARTILLERY BATTERY

### 36.  MISSISSIPPI SEVEN STARS ARTILLERY BATTERY
*Organization:*  Organized in early 1862.  It was armed with three 6-lb. Smoothbores, one 6-lb. Howitzers, and two 6-lb. Rifles on October 24, 1862. Surrendered at Port Hudson, Louisiana on July 8, 1863.  Paroled in July 1863. The uncaptured section was armed with one 6-lb. Smoothbore and one 12-lb. Howitzer on January 5, 1864.  No record after March 20, 1864.
*First Commander:*  Calvit Roberts (Captain)
*Assignments:*  Port Hudson, Department #1 (April-June 1862)
Port Hudson, Department of Southern Mississippi and East Louisiana (June-July 1862)
1st Sub-district, District of the Mississippi, Department #2 (July-October 1862)
1st Sub-district, Department of Mississippi and East Louisiana (October 1862)
3rd Military District, Department of Mississippi and East Louisiana (October 1862-January 1863)
Maxey's Brigade, 3rd Military District, Department of Mississippi and East Louisiana (January-May 1863)
Miles' Brigade, 3rd Military District, Department of Mississippi and East Louisiana (May-July 1863)
Logan's Cavalry Brigade, 3rd Military District, Department of Mississippi and East Louisiana [section] (March-September 1863)
Logan's Cavalry Brigade, Department of Mississippi and East Louisiana [section] (September-November 1863)
Griffith's-W. Adams' Brigade, Jackson's Division, Lee's Cavalry Corps, Department of Mississippi and East Louisiana [section] (November 1863-January 1864)
W. Adams' Brigade, Jackson's Division, Lee's Cavalry Corps, Department of Alabama, Mississippi, and East Louisiana [section] (January-March 1864)
*Battles:*  Port Hudson Siege (May-July 1863)
Expedition toward Canton [section] (October 14-20, 1863)
Meridian Campaign (February-March 1864)

## 37. MISSISSIPPI SMITH'S-TURNER'S ARTILLERY BATTERY

*Organization:* Organized on July 1, 1861. It was armed with four 6-lb. Smoothbores on October 8, 1862. It was armed with two 6-lb. Smoothbores and two 12-lb. Howitzers from October 8, 1862 to December 31, 1862. It was armed with four 12-lb. Napoleons from December 31, 1862 to April 1, 1864. Surrendered by Lieutenant General Richard Taylor, commanding the Department of Alabama, Mississippi, and East Louisiana, at Citronelle, Alabama on May 4, 1865.

*First Commander:* Melancthon Smith (Captain)

*Captain:* William B. Turner

*Assignments:* Cheatham's Brigade, 1st Geographical Division, Department #2 (September-October 1861)

Stephens' Brigade, Cheatham's Division, 1st Geographical Division, Department #2 (October 1861-March 1862)

Stephens' Brigade, 1st Grand Division, Army of the Mississippi, Department #2 (March 1862)

Stephens'-Maney's Brigade, Cheatham's Division, 1st Corps, Army of the Mississippi, Department #2 (March-July 1862)

Maney's Brigade, Cheatham's Division, Army of the Mississippi, Department #2 (July-August 1862)

Maney's Brigade, Cheatham's Division, Right Wing, Army of the Mississippi, Department #2 (August-November 1862)

Maney's Brigade, Cheatham's Division, 1st Corps, Army of Tennessee (November 1862-August 1863)

Artillery Battalion, Cheatham's Division, 1st Corps, Army of Tennessee (August 1863-February 1864)

Hoxton's Battalion, Artillery, 1st Corps, Army of Tennessee (February 1864-January 1865)

Gee's Artillery Battalion, Right Wing, Defenses of Mobile, Artillery Reserves, etc., District of the Gulf, Department of Alabama, Mississippi, and East Louisiana (March-April 1865)

3rd Battalion, Smith's Artillery Regiment, Department of Alabama, Mississippi, and East Louisiana (April-May 1865)

*Battles:* Belmont (November 7, 1861)

Shiloh (April 6-7, 1862)

Corinth Campaign (April-June 1862)

Perryville (October 8, 1862)

Murfreesboro (December 31, 1862-January 3, 1863)

Chickamauga (September 19-20, 1863)

Chattanooga Siege (September-November 1863)

Chattanooga (November 23-25, 1863)

Atlanta Campaign (May-September 1864)
Atlanta Siege (July-September 1864)
Nashville (December 15-16, 1864)
Mobile (March 17-April 12, 1865)

## 38. MISSISSIPPI SPENCER'S ARTILLERY BATTERY
*See:* KENTUCKY ISSAQUENA ARTILLERY BATTERY

## 39. MISSISSIPPI STANFORD'S ARTILLERY BATTERY
**Organization:** Organized at Grenada on May 17, 1861. It was armed with four 12-lb. Napoleons from March 29, 1864 to April 1, 1864. Apparently disbanded in December 1864.
**First Commander:** Thomas J. Stanford (Captain)
**Assignments:** Tappan's Brigade, 2nd Division, 1st Geographical Division, Department #2 (January-March 1862)
Tappan's Brigade, 1st Grand Division, Army of the Mississippi, Department #2 (March 1862)
Stewart's Brigade, Clark's Division, 1st Corps, Army of the Mississippi, Department #2 (March-July 1862)
Stewart's Brigade, Cheatham's Division, Army of the Mississippi, Department #2 (July-August 1862)
Stewart's Brigade, Cheatham's Division, Right Wing, Army of the Mississippi, Department #2 (August-November 1862)
Stewart's-Strahl's Brigade, Cheatham's Division, 1st Corps, Army of Tennessee (November 1862-August 1863)
Artillery Battalion, Cheatham's Division, 1st Corps, Army of Tennessee (August-November 1863)
Artillery Battalion, Stewart's Division, 2nd Corps, Army of Tennessee (November 1863-February 1864)
Eldridge's Battalion, Artillery, 2nd Corps, Army of Tennessee (February-December 1864)
**Battles:** Shiloh (April 6-7, 1862)
Corinth Campaign (April-June 1862)
Perryville (October 8, 1862)
Murfreesboro (December 31, 1862-January 3, 1863)
Tullahoma Campaign (June 1863)
Chickamauga (September 19-20, 1863)
Chattanooga Siege (September-November 1863)
Chattanooga (November 23-25, 1863)
Atlanta Campaign (May-September 1864)
New Hope Church (May 25-June 4, 1864)

Atlanta Siege (July-September 1864)
Nashville (December 15-16, 1864)

## 40. MISSISSIPPI SWINDOLL'S ARTILLERY BATTERY

*Organization:* Organized in the fall of 1863. Apparently disbanded shortly thereafter.
*First Commander:* W. C. Swindoll, Jr. (Captain)
*Assignment:* Logan's Cavalry Brigade, Department of Mississippi and East Louisiana (October 1863)
*Battle:* Expedition toward Canton (October 14-20, 1863)

## 41. MISSISSIPPI TULL'S ARTILLERY BATTERY

*Organization:* Organized at Vicksburg, Warren County in April 1861. Apparently failed to complete its organization.
*First Commander:* F. S. Tull (Captain)

## 42. MISSISSIPPI VAIDEN ARTILLERY BATTERY

*See:* MISSISSIPPI 1ST LIGHT ARTILLERY REGIMENT, COMPANY L

## 43. MISSISSIPPI WARREN LIGHT ARTILLERY BATTERY

*Organization:* Organized on May 1, 1861. Mustered into Confederate service in August 1861. It was armed with four 6-lb. Smoothbores and two 12-lb. Howitzers on April 6-7, 1862. It was armed with three 12-lb. Napoleons on March 29-April 1, 1864. Surrendered by General Joseph E. Johnston at Durham Station, Orange County, North Carolina on April 26, 1865.
*First Commander:* Charles Swett (Captain)
*Assignments:* Artillery, Hardee's Division, Central Army of Kentucky, Department #2 (October 1861-January 1862)
Hindman's Brigade, Hardee's Division, Central Army of Kentucky, Department #2 (January-March 1862)
Hindman's-Shaver's Brigade, 3rd Corps, Army of the Mississippi, Department #2 (March-May 1862)
Marmaduke's Brigade, 3rd Corps, Army of the Mississippi, Department #2 (June-July 1862)
Marmaduke's Brigade, Buckner's Division, Army of the Mississippi, Department #2 (July-August 1862)
Liddell's Brigade, Buckner's Division, 2nd Corps, Army of the Mississippi, Department #2 (August-November 1862)
Liddell's Brigade, Buckner's-Cleburne's Division, 2nd Corps, Army of Tennessee (November 1862-August 1863)

Artillery Battalion, Cleburne's Division, 2nd Corps, Army of Tennessee (August-September 1863)

Artillery Battalion, Liddell's Division, Reserve Corps, Army of Tennessee (September 1863)

Artillery Battalion, Cleburne's Division, 2nd Corps, Army of Tennessee (September-November 1863)

Artillery Battalion, Cleburne's Division, 1st Corps, Army of Tennessee (November 1863-February 1864)

Hotchkiss' Battalion, Artillery, 1st Corps, Army of Tennessee (February-September 1864)

Hotchkiss' Artillery Battalion, Macon, Georgia, Department of Tennessee (September 1864)

Palmer's Artillery Battalion, Unattached, Army of Tennessee (April 1865)

**Battles:**  Brownsville (November 20, 1861)

Rowlett's Station (December 17, 1861)

Woodsonville (December 17, 1861)

Shiloh (April 6-7, 1862)

Corinth (October 3-4, 1862)

Farmington (May 1862)

Perryville (October 8, 1862)

Murfreesboro (December 31, 1862-January 3, 1863)

Tullahoma Campaign (June 1863)

Liberty Gap (June 24, 1863)

Chickamauga (September 19-20, 1863)

Chattanooga Siege (September-November 1863)

Chattanooga (November 23-25, 1863)

Atlanta Campaign (May-September 1864)

Atlanta Siege (July-September 1864)

Carolinas Campaign (February-April 1865)

## 44.    MISSISSIPPI WESSON ARTILLERY BATTERY, LOCAL DEFENSE TROOPS

**Organization:**  Organized in 1863.  No further record.
**First Commander:**  J. C. Kittrell (Captain)

# CAVALRY

### 45. MISSISSIPPI 1ST CAVALRY BATTALION

*Organization:* Organized in the summer of 1861. Became part of Lindsay's [Improvised] Mississippi Cavalry Regiment on April 2, 1862.
*First Commander:* John H. Miller (Major, Lieutenant Colonel)
*Field Officer:* E. L. Hankins (Major)
*Assignments:* Unattached, 1st Geographical Division, Department #2 (September-October 1861)
Cavalry, Cheatham's Division, 1st Geographical Division, Department #2 (October 1861)
Cavalry, Polk's Division, 1st Geographical Division, Department #2 (November 1861)
Unattached, 1st Geographical Division, Department #2 (January-March 1862)
Unattached, 1st Grand Division, Army of the Mississippi, Department #2 (March 1862)
Cavalry, 1st Corps, Army of the Mississippi, Department #2 (March-April 1862)
*Battles:* Underwood's Farm, near Bird's Point [Company A] (October 14, 1861)
Belmont (November 7, 1861)
near Fort Heiman [skirmish] (February 13, 1862)

### 46. MISSISSIPPI 1ST CAVALRY BATTALION, STATE TROOPS

*Also Known As:* 1st Cavalry Battalion, Minute Men
*Organization:* Organized for six months in early 1863. Apparently reorganized as the 1st Cavalry Regiment, State Troops, in April or May 1863.
*First Commander:* Green L. Blythe (Major)
*Assignment:* 5th Military District, Department of Mississippi and East Louisiana (February-April 1863)

**Battle:** Operations along the Memphis and Charleston Railroad (May 19-July 4, 1863)

## 47. MISSISSIPPI 1ST CAVALRY REGIMENT

**Organization:** Organized in mid-1862. Surrendered by Lieutenant General Richard Taylor, commanding the Department of Alabama, Mississippi, and East Louisiana, at Meridian, Mississippi on May 4, 1865.

**First Commander:** Jules C. Denis (Colonel)

**Field Officers:** Richard A. Pinson (Colonel)

John H. Miller (Major, Lieutenant Colonel)

Franklin A. Montgomery (Lieutenant Colonel)

John S. Simmons (Major)

E. G. Wheeler (Major)

**Assignments:** 3rd Sub-district, District of the Mississippi, Department #2 (July-August 1862)

2nd Sub-district, District of the Mississippi, Department #2 (September 1862)

Cavalry Brigade, 1st Division, District of the Mississippi, Army of West Tennessee, Department #2 (September-October 1862)

Cavalry Brigade, 1st Division, District of the Mississippi, Army of West Tennessee, Department of Mississippi and East Louisiana (October 1862)

Cavalry, 1st Corps, Army of West Tennessee, Department of Mississippi and East Louisiana (November-December 1862)

Cavalry Corps, Army of North Mississippi, Department of Mississippi and East Louisiana (December 1862-January 1863)

Cosby's Brigade, Jackson's Division, Van Dorn's Cavalry Corps, Department of Mississippi and East Louisiana (January-February 1863)

Cosby's Brigade, Martin's Division, Van Dorn's Cavalry Corps, Department of Mississippi and East Louisiana (February 1863)

Cosby's Brigade, Martin's Division, Van Dorn's Cavalry Corps, Army of Tennessee (March-May 1863)

Cosby's Brigade, Jackson's Cavalry Division, Army of the West, Trans-Mississippi Department (June-July 1863)

Cosby's Brigade, Jackson's Cavalry Division, Department of Mississippi and East Louisiana (July-August 1863)

Jackson's Brigade, Jackson's Division, Lee's Cavalry Corps, Department of Mississippi and East Louisiana (August-September 1863)

Ross' Brigade, Jackson's Division, Lee's Cavalry Corps, Department of Mississippi and East Louisiana (September-December 1863)

Starke's-Cosby's Brigade, Jackson's Division, Lee's Cavalry Corps, Department of Mississippi and East Louisiana (December 1863-January 1864)

Cosby's-Starke's Brigade, Jackson's Division, Department of Alabama, Mississippi, and East Louisiana (January-May 1864)

Starke's-Armstrong's Brigade, Jackson's Cavalry Division, Army of Mississippi (May-July 1864)

Armstrong's Brigade, Jackson's Cavalry Division, Army of Tennessee (July 1864-January 1865)

Armstrong's Brigade, Jackson's Division, Forrest's Cavalry Corps, Department of Alabama, Mississippi, and East Louisiana (January-February 1865)

Armstrong's Brigade, Chalmers' Division, Forrest's Cavalry Corps, Department of Alabama, Mississippi, and East Louisiana (February-May 1865)

**Battles:**  Expedition from Holly Springs, Mississippi to Bolivar and Jackson, Tennessee [detachment] (July 25-August 1, 1862)

Corinth (October 3-4, 1862)

near Lamar (November 6, 1862)

Hudsonville (November 8, 1862)

Holly Springs (December 20, 1862)

Thompson's Station (March 5, 1863)

*vs. Barataria*, Amite River [detachment] (April 7, 1863)

Amite River [Company H] (April 12, 1863)

Vicksburg Campaign (May-July 1863)

Jackson Siege (July 1863)

Meridian Campaign (February-March 1864)

Atlanta Campaign (May-September 1864)

Atlanta Siege (July-September 1864)

Campbellton (July 28, 1864)

Franklin-Nashville Campaign (November 1864-January 1865)

Wilson's Raid (March-April 1865)

Selma (April 2, 1865)

**Further Reading:**  Bowman, Thornton Hardie, *Reminiscences of an ex-Confederate Solider*. Montgomery, Franklin Alexander, *Reminiscences of a Mississippian in Peace and War*.

## 48.  MISSISSIPPI 1ST (W. ADAMS') CAVALRY REGIMENT
*See:* MISSISSIPPI W. ADAMS'-WOOD'S CAVALRY REGIMENT

## 49.  MISSISSIPPI 1ST (LINDSAY'S) CAVALRY REGIMENT
*See:* MISSISSIPPI LINDSAY'S [IMPROVISED] CAVALRY REGIMENT

## 50.  MISSISSIPPI 1ST CAVALRY REGIMENT, PARTISAN RANGERS
*Also Known As:*  7th Cavalry Regiment

**Organization:**  Organized in mid-1862. Part of the regiment was in a field organization with the 8th Cavalry Regiment from February 18, 1865 to May 4, 1865. This portion was surrendered by Lieutenant General Richard Taylor, commanding the Department of Alabama, Mississippi, and East Louisiana, at Meridian, Mississippi on May 4, 1865. The balance of the regiment was in a field organization with the 28th Cavalry Regiment from February 18, 1865 to May 4, 1865. Consolidated with the 3rd Cavalry Regiment and part of the 14th Confederate Cavalry Regiment and designated as the 3rd, 14th (Confederate), and 28th Cavalry Regiment Consolidated in February 1865.

**First Commander:**  William C. Falkner (Colonel)

**Field Officers:**  W. L. Davis (Major)

Lawson B. Hovis (Lieutenant Colonel)

Samuel M. Hyams, Jr. (Lieutenant Colonel)

James M. Park (Major, Lieutenant Colonel)

William N. Stansell (Major)

**Assignments:**  3rd Sub-district, District of the Mississippi, Department #2 (July-September 1862)

Unattached, Army of West Tennessee, Department #2 (September 1862)

Armstrong's Cavalry Brigade, Price's Corps, Army of West Tennessee, Department #2 (September-October 1862)

Armstrong's Cavalry Brigade, Price's Corps, Army of West Tennessee, Department of Mississippi and East Louisiana (October-December 1862)

Cavalry, Price's Corps, Army of North Mississippi, Department of Mississippi and East Louisiana (December 1862-January 1863)

5th Military District, Department of Mississippi and East Louisiana (January-September 1863)

Chalmers' Cavalry Brigade, Department of Mississippi and East Louisiana (September-October 1863)

McCulloch's Brigade, Chalmers' Division, Lee's Cavalry Corps, Department of Mississippi and East Louisiana (October 1863-January 1864)

McCulloch's Brigade, Chalmers' Division, Forrest's Cavalry Corps, Department of Mississippi and East Louisiana (January 1864)

McCulloch's Brigade, Chalmers' Division, Forrest's Cavalry Corps, Department of Alabama, Mississippi, and East Louisiana (January-September 1864)

McCulloch's Cavalry Brigade, District of the Gulf, Department of Alabama, Mississippi, and East Louisiana (September 1864-January 1865)

Starke's Brigade, Chalmers' Division, Forrest's Cavalry Corps, Department of Alabama, Mississippi, and East Louisiana (February-May 1865)

**Battles:**  Peyton's Mill (September 19, 1862)

Iuka (September 19, 1862)

near Ripley (November 20, 1862)

Operations along the Memphis and Charleston Railroad (May 19-July 4, 1863)
Chalmers' Raid in West Tennessee and North Mississippi (October 4-17, 1863)
Colliersville (November 3, 1863)
A.J. Smith's 2nd Mississippi Invasion (August 1864)
Tupelo (July 14, 1864)
Wilson's Raid (March-April 1865)

### 51. MISSISSIPPI 1ST CAVALRY REGIMENT, RESERVES

*Organization:*  Organized in August 1864.  Surrendered by Lieutenant General Richards Taylor, commanding the Department of Alabama, Mississippi, and East Louisiana, at Meridian, Mississippi on May 4, 1865.
*First Commander:*  Jules C. Denis (Colonel)
*Field Officers:*  J. F. Mesten (Major)
David W. Metts (Lieutenant Colonel)
*Assignments:*  Denis' Cavalry Brigade, Northern Sub-district, District of Mississippi and East Louisiana, Department of Alabama, Mississippi, and East Louisiana (August 1864-February 1865)
Denis' Cavalry Brigade, Sub-district of North Mississippi and West Tennessee, District of Mississippi and East Louisiana, Department of Alabama, Mississippi, and East Louisiana (February-May 1865)

### 52. MISSISSIPPI 1ST CAVALRY REGIMENT, STATE TROOPS

*Also Known As:*  2nd Partisan Rangers Regiment State Troops
*Organization:*  Organized by the increase of the 1st Cavalry Battalion, State Troops to a regiment 1n April or May 1863.  Temporarily disbanded for reorganization upon the expiration of the regiment's term of service ca. September 1863.  Apparently never reorganized.
*First Commander:*  Green L. Blythe (Colonel)
*Field Officers:*  C. L. Bowen (Major)
A. C. Edmondson (Lieutenant Colonel)
*Assignments:*  3rd (George's) Brigade, 5th Military District, Department of Mississippi and East Louisiana (May-September 1863)
Chalmers' Cavalry Brigade, Department of Mississippi and East Louisiana (September 1863)

### 53. MISSISSIPPI 2ND (BASKERVILLE'S) CAVALRY BATTALION
*See:* MISSISSIPPI 4TH CAVALRY BATTALION

### 54. MISSISSIPPI 2ND (MARTIN'S) CAVALRY BATTALION
*See:* MISSISSIPPI JEFF. DAVIS CAVALRY LEGION

## 55.  MISSISSIPPI [AND ALABAMA] 2ND (BREWER'S) CAVALRY BATTALION

**Organization:**  Organized with seven Alabama and Mississippi companies in late 1861. Consolidated with three companies of the 1st (Beall's) Alabama Cavalry Battalion and designated as the 8th (Wade's) Confederate Cavalry Regiment in May 1862.

**First Commander:**  Richard H. Brewer (Major)

**Field Officer:**  W. N. Mercer (Major)

**Assignments:**  Unattached, 1st Geographical Division, Department #2 (January-March 1862)

Unattached, 1st Grand Division, Army of the Mississippi, Department #2 (March 1862)

Cavalry, 1st Corps, Army of the Mississippi, Department #2 (March-April 1862)

Beall's Cavalry Brigade, Department #2 (April-May 1862)

**Battles:**  Expedition toward Purdy and operations about Crump's Landing (March 9-14, 1862)

Shiloh (April 6-7, 1862)

Corinth Campaign (April-June 1862)

## 56.  MISSISSIPPI 2ND CAVALRY BATTALION, RESERVES

**Organization:**  Organized in 1864. Surrendered by Lieutenant General Richard Taylor, commanding the Department of Alabama, Mississippi, and East Louisiana, at Meridian, Mississippi on May 4, 1865.

**Assignments:**  Denis' Cavalry Brigade, Northern Sub-district, District of Mississippi and East Louisiana, Department of Alabama, Mississippi, and East Louisiana (November 1864-February 1865)

Denis' Cavalry Brigade, Sub-district of North Mississippi and West Tennessee, District of Mississippi and East Louisiana, Department of Alabama, Mississippi, and East Louisiana (February-May 1865)

## 57.  MISSISSIPPI 2ND CAVALRY BATTALION, STATE TROOPS

**Also Known As:**  2nd Cavalry Battalion, Minute Men

Harris' Cavalry Battalion, State Troops

**Organization:**  Organized for six months in the fall of 1863. Probably consolidated with the 3rd Cavalry Battalion and the 3rd Cavalry Battalion, State Troops and designated as Ashcraft's Cavalry Regiment in late 1864.

**First Commander:**  Thomas W. Harris (Major)

**Assignments:**  Richardson's Brigade, Chalmers' Division, Lee's Cavalry Corps, Department of Mississippi and East Louisiana (October 1863)

Gholson's Brigade, Forrest's Cavalry Corps, Department of Alabama, Mississippi, and East Louisiana (May 1864)

Gholson's Brigade, Buford's Division, Forrest's Cavalry Corps, Department of Alabama, Mississippi, and East Louisiana (May-June 1864)

Gholson's Brigade, W. Adams' Cavalry Division, Lee's Cavalry Corps, Department of Alabama, Mississippi, and East Louisiana (June-August 1864)

## 58. MISSISSIPPI 2ND CAVALRY REGIMENT

*Also Known As:* 42nd Cavalry Regiment

42nd Mounted Infantry Regiment

4th Cavalry Regiment

*Organization:* Organized by the increase of Gordon's Cavalry Battalion to a regiment in the summer of 1862. Surrendered by Lieutenant General Richard Taylor, commanding the Department of Alabama, Mississippi, and East Louisiana, at Citronelle, Alabama on May 4, 1865.

*First Commander:* James Gordon (Colonel)

*Field Officer:* J. L. Harris (Major)

*Assignments:* Armstrong's Cavalry Brigade, District of the Tennessee, Department #2 (August-September 1862)

Armstrong's Cavalry Brigade, Price's Corps, Army of West Tennessee, Department #2 (September-October 1862)

Armstrong's Cavalry Brigade, Price's Corps, Army of West Tennessee, Department of Mississippi and East Louisiana (October-December 1862)

Jackson's Cavalry Corps, Army of North Mississippi, Department of Mississippi and East Louisiana (December 1862)

Armstrong's Brigade, Jackson's Division, Van Dorn's Cavalry Corps, Department of Mississippi and East Louisiana (December 1862-January 1863)

1st Military District, Department of Mississippi and East Louisiana (January 1863)

Armstrong's Brigade, Jackson's Division, Van Dorn's Cavalry Corps, Department of Mississippi and East Louisiana (January-February 1863)

Armstrong's Brigade, Jackson's Division, Van Dorn's Cavalry Corps, Army of Tennessee (March 1863)

Armstrong's Brigade, Forrest's Division, Van Dorn's Cavalry Corps, Army of Tennessee (March-May 1863)

Armstrong's Brigade, Forrest's Cavalry Division, Army of Tennessee (May-June 1863)

Cosby's Brigade, Jackson's Cavalry Division, Department of the West (June-July 1863)

Cosby's Brigade, Jackson's Cavalry Division, Department of Mississippi and East Louisiana (July-August 1863)

Jackson's-Cosby's Brigade, Jackson's Division, Lee's Cavalry Corps, Department of Mississippi and East Louisiana (August-December 1863)

Provost Guard, Jackson's Division, Lee's Cavalry Corps, Department of Mississippi and East Louisiana [Company D] (September-December 1863)

Adams' Brigade, Jackson's Division, Lee's Cavalry Corps, Department of Mississippi and East Louisiana (January 1864)

Adams' Brigade, Jackson's Division, Lee's Cavalry Corps, Department of Alabama, Mississippi, and East Louisiana (January-May 1864)

Armstrong's Brigade, Jackson's Cavalry Division, Army of Mississippi (May-July 1864)

Armstrong's Brigade, Jackson's Cavalry Division, Army of Tennessee (July-November 1864)

Armstrong's Brigade, Jackson's Division, Forrest's Cavalry Corps, Army of Tennessee (November 1864-January 1865)

Armstrong's Brigade, Jackson's Division, Forrest's Cavalry Corps, Department of Alabama, Mississippi, and East Louisiana (January-February 1865)

Armstrong's Brigade, Chalmers' Division, Forrest's Cavalry Corps, Department of Alabama, Mississippi, and East Louisiana (February-May 1865)

**Battles:** Thompson's Station (March 5, 1863)

Brentwood (March 25, 1863)

Franklin (April 10, 1863)

Jackson Siege (July 1863)

Meridian Campaign (February-March 1864)

Atlanta Siege (July-September 1864)

Campbellton (July 28, 1864)

Franklin (November 30, 1864)

Wilson's Raid (March-April 1865)

## 59.  MISSISSIPPI 2ND CAVALRY REGIMENT, PARTISAN RANGERS

**Also Known As:** Ballantine's Cavalry Regiment

**Organization:** Organized in late 1862. Surrendered by Lieutenant General Richard Taylor, commanding the Department of Alabama, Mississippi, and East Louisiana, at Meridian, Mississippi on May 4, 1865.

**First Commander:** John G. Ballantine (Colonel)

**Field Officers:** William H. Ford (Major)

William L. Maxwell (Major, Lieutenant Colonel)

**Assignments:** Jackson's Cavalry Corps, Army of North Mississippi, Department of Mississippi and East Louisiana (December 1862-January 1863)

2nd Brigade, Jackson's Division, Van Dorn's Cavalry Corps, Department of Mississippi and East Louisiana (January-February 1863)

Cosby's Brigade, Martin's Division, Van Dorn's Cavalry Corps, Department of Mississippi and East Louisiana (February 1863)

Cosby's Brigade, Martin's Division, Van Dorn's Cavalry Corps, Army of Tennessee (February-May 1863)

Cosby's Brigade, Jackson's Cavalry Division, Department of the West (June-July 1863)

Cosby's Brigade, Jackson's Cavalry Division, Department of Mississippi and East Louisiana (July-August 1863)

Cosby's Brigade, Jackson's Division, Lee's Cavalry Corps, Department of Mississippi and East Louisiana (August 1863-January 1864)

Cosby's Brigade, Jackson's Division, Lee's Cavalry Corps, Department of Alabama, Mississippi, and East Louisiana (January-May 1864)

Cosby's-Armstrong's Brigade, Jackson's Cavalry Division, Army of Mississippi (May-July 1864)

Armstrong's Brigade, Jackson's Cavalry Division, Army of Tennessee (July 1864-February 1865)

Armstrong's Brigade, Chalmers' Division, Forrest's Cavalry Corps, Department of Alabama, Mississippi, and East Louisiana (February-May 1865)

**Battles:** Thompson's Station (March 5, 1863)

Vicksburg Campaign (May-July 1863)

Austin (May 24, 1863)

Jackson Siege (July 1863)

Meridian Campaign (February-March 1864)

Atlanta Campaign (May-September 1864)

Atlanta Siege (July-September 1864)

Campbellton (July 28, 1864)

Franklin-Nashville Campaign (November 1864-January 1865)

Wilson's Raid (March-April 1865)

## 60.   MISSISSIPPI 2ND CAVALRY REGIMENT, PARTISAN RANGERS, STATE TROOPS

*See:* MISSISSIPPI 1ST CAVALRY REGIMENT, STATE TROOPS

## 61.   MISSISSIPPI 2ND CAVALRY REGIMENT, STATE TROOPS

**Organization:**  Organized in the summer of 1863.  Transferred to Confederate service on April 30, 1864.  Consolidated with Ashcraft's and Ham's Cavalry Regiments and designated as Ashcraft's, Ham's, and Lowry's Cavalry Regiment Consolidated on March 20, 1865.

**First Commander:**  J. F. Smith (Colonel)

**Field Officers:**  Joseph A. Johnson (Lieutenant Colonel)

William L. Lowry (Lieutenant Colonel, Colonel)

L. L. Marshall (Major)

**Assignments:** 5th Military District, Department of Mississippi and East Louisiana (August-September 1863)

Chalmer's Cavalry Brigade, Department of Mississippi and East Louisiana (September-October 1863)

Slemmon's Brigade, Chalmers' Cavalry Division, Department of Mississippi and East Louisiana (October-November 1863)

Slemmon's Brigade, Chalmers' Division, Lee's Cavalry Corps, Department of Mississippi and East Louisiana (November 1863)

Gholson's Brigade, Forrest's Cavalry Corps, Department of Alabama, Mississippi, and East Louisiana (May-June 1864)

Gholson's Brigade, W. Adams' Cavalry Division, Department of Alabama, Mississippi, and East Louisiana (June-August 1864)

Armstrong's Brigade, Chalmers' Division, Forrest's Cavalry Corps, Department of Alabama, Mississippi, and East Louisiana (February-March 1865)

**Battles:** Vicksburg Campaign (May-July 1863)

Grierson's Raid (April 17-May 2, 1863)

## 62. MISSISSIPPI 3RD CAVALRY BATTALION

**Organization:** This battalion does not appear in the *Official Records*. It apparently was consolidated with the 2nd and 3rd Cavalry Battalion, State Troops and was designated as Ashcraft's Mississippi Cavalry Regiment in 1864.

**First Commander:** E. L. Hankins (Major)

## 63. MISSISSIPPI 3RD CAVALRY BATTALION, RESERVES

**Organization:** Organized in the fall of 1864. Surrendered by Lieutenant General Richard Taylor, commanding the Department of Alabama, Mississippi, and East Louisiana, at Meridian, Mississippi on May 4, 1865.

**Assignments:** Denis' Cavalry Brigade, Northern Sub-district, District of Mississippi and East Louisiana, Department of Alabama, Mississippi, and East Louisiana (November 1864-February 1865)

Denis' Cavalry Brigade, Sub-district of North Mississippi and West Tennessee, District of Mississippi and East Louisiana, Department of Alabama, Mississippi, and East Louisiana (February-May 1865)

## 64. MISSISSIPPI 3RD CAVALRY BATTALION, STATE TROOPS

**Organization:** Organized in 1863. Probably consolidated with the 3rd Cavalry Battalion and the 2nd Cavalry Battalion, State Troops and designated as Ashcraft's Cavalry Regiment in 1864.

**First Commander:** Thomas C. Ashcraft (Lieutenant Colonel)

## 65. MISSISSIPPI 3RD CAVALRY REGIMENT

**Organization:** Organized by the transfer of the 3rd Cavalry Regiment, State Troops to Confederate service on April 30, 1864. Dismounted in the spring of 1864. Consolidated with part of the 14th Confederate Cavalry Regiment and the 28th Mississippi Cavalry Regiment and designated as the 3rd, 14th (Confederate), and 28th Mississippi Cavalry Regiment Consolidated in February 1865.

**First Commander:** John McGuirk (Colonel)

**Field Officers:** Hickerson H. Barksdale (Lieutenant Colonel)

Thomas W. Webb (Major)

**Assignments:** Gholson's Brigade, Forrest's Cavalry Corps, Department of Alabama, Mississippi, and East Louisiana (April-June 1864)

Gholson's Brigade, Adams' Cavalry Division, Department of Alabama, Mississippi, and East Louisiana (June-August 1864)

Reynolds' Brigade, Cantey's Division, 3rd Corps, Army of Tennessee (August 1864-February 1865)

**Battles:** Atlanta Campaign (May-September 1864)

Atlanta Siege (July-September 1864)

## 66. MISSISSIPPI 3RD CAVALRY REGIMENT, STATE TROOPS

**Organization:** Organized in the spring of 1863. Transferred to Confederate service on April 30, 1864.

**First Commander:** John McGuirk (Colonel)

**Field Officers:** James A. Barksdale (Lieutenant Colonel)

Benjamin M. Kilgore (Major)

**Assignments:** George's Brigade, 5th Military District, Department of Mississippi and East Louisiana (May-August 1863)

5th Military District, Department of Mississippi and East Louisiana (August-September 1863)

Chalmers' Cavalry Brigade, Department of Mississippi and East Louisiana (September-October 1863)

Slemons' Brigade, Chalmers' Cavalry Division, Department of Mississippi and East Louisiana (October-November 1863)

Slemons' Brigade, Chalmers' Division, Lee's Cavalry Corps, Department of Mississippi and East Louisiana (November 1863-January 1864)

Slemons' Brigade, Chalmers' Division, Lee's Cavalry Corps, Department of Alabama, Mississippi, and East Louisiana (January-March 1864)

**Battles:** Operations along the Memphis and Charleston Railroad (May 19-July 4, 1863)

Chalmers' Raid in West Tennessee and North Mississippi (October 4-17, 1863)

Colliersville (November 3, 1863)

La Grange (February 2, 1864)

## 67.   MISSISSIPPI 3RD, 14TH (CONFEDERATE), AND 28TH CONSOLIDATED CAVALRY REGIMENT

**Organization:**  Organized by the consolidation of the 3rd and 28th Cavalry Regiments and part of the 14th Confederate Cavalry Regiment in early 1865. The six Mississippi companies of the 14th Confederate Cavalry Regiment were consolidated into two companies and assigned as Companies C and H of this regiment.  Surrendered by Lieutenant General Richard Taylor, commanding the Department of Alabama, Mississippi, and East Louisiana, at Citronelle, Alabama on May 4, 1865.

**Assignment:**  Adams' Brigade, Chalmers' Division, Forrest's Cavalry Corps, Department of Alabama, Mississippi, and East Louisiana (February-May 1865)

**Battle:**  Wilson's Raid (March-April 1865)   ·

## 68.   MISSISSIPPI 4TH CAVALRY BATTALION

**Also Known As:**  2nd Cavalry Battalion

**Organization:**  Organized in the fall of 1861.  Apparently disbanded in the spring of 1862.

**First Commander:**  Charles Baskerville (Lieutenant Colonel)

**Assignments:**  Central Army of Kentucky, Department #2 (December 1861-March 1862)

Chalmers' Brigade, 1st Corps, 2nd Grand Division, Army of the Mississippi, Department #2 (March 1862)

## 69.   MISSISSIPPI 4TH CAVALRY REGIMENT

**Organization:**  Organized by the consolidation of Hughes' Cavalry Battalion, Partisan Rangers and Stockdale's Cavalry Battalion in November 1863.  Surrendered by Lieutenant General Richard Taylor, commanding the Department of Alabama, Mississippi, and East Louisiana, at Meridian, Mississippi on May 4, 1865.

**First Commander:**  Christopher C. Wilbourn (Colonel)

**Field Officers:**  Cornelius McLaurin (Lieutenant Colonel)

James M. Norman (Major)

Thomas R. Stockdale (Major, Lieutenant Colonel)

**Assignments:**  Logan's-Griffith's-W. Adams' Brigade, Jackson's Division, Lee's Cavalry Corps, Department of Mississippi and East Louisiana (November 1863-January 1864)

W. Adams' Brigade, Jackson's Division, Lee's Cavalry Corps, Department of Alabama, Mississippi, and East Louisiana (January-May 1864)

Mabry's Brigade, W. Adams' Cavalry Division, Department of Alabama, Mississippi, and East Louisiana (May-August 1864)

Mabry's Cavalry Brigade, District North of Homochitto [W. Adams' Division], Department of Alabama, Mississippi, and East Louisiana (August-October 1864)

Mabry's Cavalry Brigade, Northern Sub-district, District of Mississippi and East Louisiana (November 1864-February 1865)

Starke's Brigade, Chalmer's Division, Forrest's Cavalry Corps, Department of Alabama, Mississippi, and East Louisiana (February-May 1865)

**Battles:** Meridian Campaign (February-March 1864)

Tupelo (July 14, 1864)

A. J. Smith's 2nd Mississippi Invasion (August 1864)

Concord Church (December 1, 1864)

Wilson's Raid (March-April 1865)


## 70. MISSISSIPPI 5TH CAVALRY REGIMENT

**Organization:** Organized by the increase of the 19th (George') Cavalry Battalion, State Troops to a regiment in the fall of 1863. Companies C, D, E, H, & K in field consolidation with the 18th Cavalry Regiment from February 18, 1865 to May 4, 1865. Surrendered by Lieutenant General Richard Taylor, commanding the Department of Alabama, Mississippi, and East Louisiana, at Meridian, Mississippi on May 4, 1865.

**First Commander:** James Z. George (Colonel)

**Field Officers:** James A. Barksdale (Lieutenant Colonel)

P. H. Echols (Major)

William G. Henderson (Major)

William T. Nesbit (Lieutenant Colonel)

William B. Peery (Major)

Wiley M. Reed (Lieutenant Colonel)

Nathaniel Wickliffe (Lieutenant Colonel)

**Assignments:** Slemons' Brigade, Chalmers' Division, Lee's Cavalry Corps, Department of Mississippi and East Louisiana (October 1863-January 1864)

Slemon's Brigade, Chalmers' Division, Lee's Cavalry Corps, Department of Alabama, Mississippi, and East Louisiana (January-March 1864)

McCulloch's-Wade's-McCulloch's Brigade, Chalmers' Division, Forrest's Cavalry Corps, Department of Alabama, Mississippi, and East Louisiana (March-September 1864)

Unattached, Chalmers' Division, Forrest's Cavalry Corps, Department of Alabama, Mississippi, and East Louisiana (September-October 1864)

Mabry's Brigade, Northern Sub-district, District of Mississippi and East Louisiana, Department of Alabama, Mississippi, and East Louisiana (November 1864-February 1865)

Armstrong's Brigade, Chalmers' Division, Forrest's Cavalry Corps, Department of Alabama, Mississippi, and East Louisiana [Companies A, B, F, G & I] (February-May 1865)

Starke's Brigade, Chalmers' Division, Forrest's Cavalry Corps, Department of Alabama, Mississippi, and East Louisiana [Companies C, D, E, H & K] (February-May 1865)

**Battles:** Chalmers' Raid in West Tennessee and North Mississippi (October 4-17, 1863)

Colliersville (November 3, 1863)

Tupelo (July 14, 1864)

A.J. Smith's 2nd Mississippi Invasion (August 1864)

Abbeville (August 23, 1864)

Nashville (December 15-16, 1864)

Wilson's Raid (March-April 1865)

## 71. MISSISSIPPI 6TH CAVALRY BATTALION, STATE TROOPS

*Organization:* Organized in the summer of 1863. Mustered out in August 1863.

*Assignment:* 5th Military District, Department of Mississippi and East Louisiana (August 1863)

## 72. MISSISSIPPI 6TH CAVALRY REGIMENT

*Organization:* Organized in early 1864. Field consolidation with the 8th Confederate Cavalry Regiment from February 18, 1865 to May 4, 1865. Surrendered by Lieutenant General Richard Taylor, commanding the Department of Alabama, Mississippi, and East Louisiana, at Meridian, Mississippi on May 4, 1865.

*First Commander:* Isham Harrison, Jr. (Colonel)

*Field Officers:* R. G. Brown (Major)

Thomas C. Lipscomb (Major, Lieutenant Colonel)

Thomas M. Nelson (Lieutenant Colonel)

*Assignments:* Ruggles' Command, Department of Alabama, Mississippi, and East Louisiana (February 1864)

Harrison's Cavalry Brigade, Ruggles' Command, Department of Alabama, Mississippi, and East Louisiana (February 1864)

Mabry's Brigade, W. Adams' Cavalry Division, Department of Alabama, Mississippi, and East Louisiana (June-August 1864)

Mabry's Cavalry Brigade, District North of Homochitto [W. Adams' Division],
Department of Alabama, Mississippi, and East Louisiana (August-October
1864)

Mabry's Cavalry Brigade, Northern Sub-district, District of Mississippi and East
Louisiana (November 1864-February 1865)

Starke's Brigade, Chalmers' Division, Forrest's Cavalry Corps, Department of
Alabama, Mississippi, and East Louisiana (February-May 1865)

**Battles:**  Tupelo (July 14, 1864)

A.J. Smith's 2nd Mississippi Invasion (August 1864)

Wilson's Raid (March-April 1865)

## 73.  MISSISSIPPI 7TH CAVALRY REGIMENT

*See:* MISSISSIPPI 1ST CAVALRY REGIMENT, PARTISAN RANGERS

## 74.  MISSISSIPPI 8TH CAVALRY REGIMENT

**Organization:**  Organized by the increase of the 19th (Duff's) Cavalry Battal-
ion to a regiment in May 1864. Regimental organization confirmed by the War
Department on July 19, 1864, per S.O. #169, Adjutant and Inspector General's
Office.  Field consolidation with part of the 1st Cavalry Regiment, Partisan
Rangers from February 18, 1865 to May 4, 1865. Surrendered by Lieutenant
General Richard Taylor, commanding the Department of Alabama, Missis-
sippi, and East Louisiana, at Meridian, Mississippi on May 4, 1865.

**First Commander:**  William L. Duff (Colonel)

**Field Officers:**  Thomas A. Mitchell (Major)

William L. Walker (Major, Lieutenant Colonel)

**Assignments:**  McCulloch's Brigade, Chalmers' Division, Forrest's Cavalry
Corps, Department of Alabama, Mississippi, and East Louisiana (May-June
1864)

Unattached, Chalmers' Division, Forrest's Cavalry Corps, Department of Alabama, Mississippi, and East Louisiana (June 1864)

Rucker's Brigade, Buford's Division, Forrest's Cavalry Corps, Department of
Alabama, Mississippi, and East Louisiana (June 1864)

Rucker's Brigade, Chalmers' Division, Forrest's Cavalry Corps, Department of
Alabama, Mississippi, and East Louisiana (June-July 1864)

Wade's-McCulloch's Brigade, Chalmers' Division, Forrest's Cavalry Corps,
Department of Alabama, Mississippi, and East Louisiana (July-September
1864)

McCulloch's Cavalry Brigade, District of the Gulf, Department of Alabama,
Mississippi, and East Louisiana (September-December 1864)

Starke's Brigade, Chalmers' Division, Forrest's Cavalry Corps, Department of
Alabama, Mississippi, and East Louisiana (February-May 1865)

**Battles:**   Sturgis' Mississippi Expedition (June 1-13, 1864)
Brice's Crossroads (June 10, 1864)
Tupelo (July 14, 1864)
A.J. Smith's 2nd Mississippi Invasion (August 1864)
Wilson's Raid (March-April 1865)

## 75.   MISSISSIPPI 9TH CAVALRY REGIMENT

**Organization:**   Organized by the increase of the 17th Cavalry Battalion, Partisan Rangers to a regiment in early 1864. Surrendered as part of Jefferson Davis' escort at Forsyth, Georgia in May 1865.

**First Commander:**   Horace H. Miller (Colonel)

**Field Officers:**   Edward J. Sanders (Major)

Abner C. Steede (Lieutenant Colonel)

**Assignments:**   Ferguson's Brigade, Jackson's Division, Lee's Cavalry Corps, Department of Alabama, Mississippi, and East Louisiana (March-May 1864)

Ferguson's Brigade, Jackson's Cavalry Division, Army of Mississippi (May-July 1864)

Ferguson's Brigade, Jackson's Cavalry Division, Army of Tennessee (July-October 1864)

Ferguson's Brigade, Iverson's-Young's Division, Wheeler's Cavalry Corps, Department of South Carolina, Georgia, and Florida (November 1864-February 1865)

Ferguson's Brigade, Young's Division, Wheeler's Cavalry Corps, Hampton's Cavalry Command (February-April 1865)

Ferguson's Brigade, Young's Division, Wheeler's Cavalry Corps, Hampton's Cavalry Command, Army of Tennessee (April 1865)

Jefferson Davis' Escort (April-May 1865)

**Battles:**   Meridian Campaign (February-March 1864)
Atlanta Campaign (May-September 1864)
Atlanta Siege (July-September 1864)
Savannah Campaign (November-December 1864)
Carolinas Campaign (February-April 1865)
Bentonville (March 19-21, 1865)

## 76.   MISSISSIPPI 10TH CAVALRY REGIMENT

**Also Known As:**   12th Cavalry Regiment

**Organization:**   Organized by the addition of Company G, 56th Alabama Mounted Infantry Regiment to the 12th Mississippi Cavalry Battalion on January 17, 1865, per S.O. #13, Adjutant and Inspector General's Office. Surrendered by General Joseph E. Johnston at Durham Station, Orange County, North Carolina on April 26, 1865.

*First Commander:* William M. Inge (Colonel)

*Assignments:* Ferguson's Brigade, Iverson's-Young's Division, Wheeler's Cavalry Corps, Department of South Carolina, Georgia, and Florida (January-February 1865)

Ferguson's Brigade, Iverson's-Young's Division, Wheeler's Cavalry Corps, Hampton's Cavalry Command (February-April 1865)

Ferguson's Brigade, Young's Division, Wheeler's Cavalry Corps, Hampton's Cavalry Command, Army of Tennessee (April 1865)

*Battles:* Carolinas Campaign (February-April 1865)

Bentonville (March 19-21, 1865)


## 77.  Mississippi 11th Cavalry Regiment

*Organization:* Organized by the increase of Perrin's Cavalry Battalion, State Troops to a regiment in the spring of 1864. Included in the surrendered of General Joseph E. Johnston at Durham Station, Orange County, North Carolina on April 26, 1865.

*First Commander:* Robert O. Perrin (Colonel)

*Field Officers:* Henry L. Muldrow (Lieutenant Colonel)

Absalom Reed (Major)

*Assignments:* Ferguson's Brigade, Jackson's Cavalry Division, Army of Mississippi (May-July 1864)

Ferguson's Brigade, Jackson's Cavalry Division, Army of Tennessee (July-September 1864)

Ferguson's Brigade, Iverson's Division, Wheeler's Cavalry Corps, Department of South Carolina, Georgia, and Florida (October 1864-February 1865)

Ferguson's Brigade, Iverson's Cavalry Division, District of Georgia and South Carolina, Department of South Carolina, Georgia, and Florida (February-April 1865)

*Battles:* Atlanta Campaign (May-September 1864)

Atlanta Siege (July-September 1864)

Savannah Campaign (November-December 1864)

Carolinas Campaign (February-April 1865)


## 78.  Mississippi 12th Cavalry Battalion

*Also Known As:* 12th Partisan Rangers Battalion

*Organization:* Organized with nine companies in early 1863. Increased to a regiment and designated as the 10th Cavalry Regiment on January 17, 1865, per S.O. #13, Adjutant and Inspector General's Office.

*First Commander:* William M. Pound (Lieutenant Colonel)

*Field Officer:* William M. Inge (Major)

*Assignments:* 1st Military District, Department of Mississippi and East Louisiana (March-August 1863)

Ferguson's Cavalry Brigade, Department of Mississippi and East Louisiana (August-October 1863)

McCulloch's Brigade, Chalmers' Cavalry Division, Department of Mississippi and East Louisiana (October-November 1863)

Ferguson's Independent Cavalry Brigade, Lee's Cavalry Corps, Department of Mississippi and East Louisiana (November 1863-January 1864)

Ferguson's Brigade, Jackson's Division, Lee's Cavalry Corps, Department of Mississippi and East Louisiana (January 1864)

Ferguson's Brigade, Jackson's Division, Lee's Cavalry Corps, Department of Alabama, Mississippi, and East Louisiana (January-May 1864)

Ferguson's Brigade, Jackson's Cavalry Division, Army of Mississippi (May-July 1864)

Ferguson's Brigade, Jackson's Cavalry Division, Army of Tennessee (July-October 1864)

Ferguson's Brigade, Iverson's-Young's Division, Wheeler's Cavalry Corps, Department of South Carolina, Georgia, and Florida (November 1864-January 1865)

*Battles:* King's Creek (May 5, 1863)

Chalmers' Raid in West Tennessee and North Mississippi (October 4-17, 1863)

Operations along the Memphis and Charleston Railroad (May 19-July 4, 1863)

Meridian Campaign (February-March 1864)

Atlanta Campaign (May-September 1864)

La Fayette (June 24, 1864)

Atlanta Siege (July-September 1864)

Savannah Campaign (November-December 1864)

Grierson's Raid (April 17-May 2, 1863)


## 79.   MISSISSIPPI 12TH CAVALRY BATTALION, PARTISAN RANGERS

*See:* MISSISSIPPI 12TH CAVALRY BATTALION


## 80.   MISSISSIPPI 12TH CAVALRY REGIMENT

*Also Known As:* 16th Confederate Cavalry Regiment

*Organization:* Organized in mid-1864. Surrendered by Lieutenant General Richard Taylor, commanding the Department of Alabama, Mississippi, and East Louisiana, at Meridian, Mississippi on May 4, 1865.

*First Commander:* Charles G. Armistead (Lieutenant Colonel)

*Field Officers:* Philip B. Spence (Lieutenant Colonel)

William Yerger, Jr. (Major)

*Assignments:* Armistead's Cavalry Brigade, District of Central and North Alabama, Department of Alabama, Mississippi, and East Louisiana (August-September 1864)

Armistead's Cavalry Brigade, District of Central Alabama, Department of Alabama, Mississippi, and East Louisiana (September 1864-March 1865)

Armistead's Cavalry Brigade, District of Alabama, Department of Alabama, Mississippi, and East Louisiana (March-May 1865)

Armstrong's Brigade, Chalmers' Division, Forrest's Cavalry Corps, Department of Alabama, Mississippi, and East Louisiana [detachment] (February-May 1865)

*Battle:* Wilson's Raid (March-April 1865)

## 81. MISSISSIPPI 12TH (INGE'S) CAVALRY REGIMENT

*See:* MISSISSIPPI 10TH CAVALRY REGIMENT

## 82. MISSISSIPPI 14TH CAVALRY BATTALION, PARTISAN RANGERS

*Also Known As:* Garland's Cavalry Battalion, Partisan Rangers

*Organization:* Organized with three companies in the fall of 1862. Became companies A, B, and C, 14th Confederate Cavalry Regiment on September 14, 1863.

*First Commander:* William H. Garland (Major)

*Assignments:* 3rd Military District, Department of Mississippi and East Louisiana (October-December 1862)

Unattached, 3rd Military District, Department of Mississippi and East Louisiana (December 1862-March 1863)

Cavalry, 3rd Military District, Department of Mississippi and East Louisiana (March-July 1863)

Logan's Cavalry Brigade, 3rd Military District, Department of Mississippi and East Louisiana (July-September 1863)

*Battles:* Grierson's Raid (April 17-May 2, 1863)

Port Hudson Siege (May-July 1863)

## 83. MISSISSIPPI 16TH CAVALRY BATTALION, STATE TROOPS

*Organization:* Organized with five companies in March 1863. Increased to a regiment, designated as Ham's Cavalry Regiment, and transferred to Confederate service on April 30, 1864.

*First Commander:* Thomas W. Ham (Major)

*Assignments:* 1st Military District, Department of Mississippi and East Louisiana (March-September 1863)

Chalmers' Cavalry Brigade, Department of Mississippi and East Louisiana (September-October 1863)

Richardson's Brigade, Chalmers' Cavalry Division, Department of Mississippi and East Louisiana (October-November 1863)

**Battle:**  Grierson's Raid (April 17-May 2, 1863)

## 84.  MISSISSIPPI 17TH CAVALRY BATTALION, PARTISAN RANGERS

**Organization:**  Organized in early 1863.  Increased to a regiment and designated as the 9th Cavalry Regiment in early 1864.

**First Commander:**  Abner C. Steede (Major)

**Assignments:**  4th Military District, Department of Mississippi and East Louisiana (February-June 1863)

Adams' Brigade, Walker's Division, Department of the West (June 1863)

Cosby's Brigade, Jackson's Cavalry Division, Department of the West (June-July 1863)

Cosby's Brigade, Jackson's Cavalry Division, Department of Mississippi and East Louisiana (July-August 1863)

Jackson's Brigade, Jackson's Cavalry Division, Department of Mississippi and East Louisiana (August 1863)

Unattached, Department of Mississippi and East Louisiana (November 1863)

**Battles:**  Vicksburg Campaign (May-July 1863)

Jackson Siege (July 1863)

## 85.  MISSISSIPPI 18TH CAVALRY BATTALION

**Organization:**  Organized in early 1863.  Increased to a regiment and designated as the 18th Cavalry Regiment ca. January 1865.

**First Commander:**  Alexander H. Chalmers (Major, Lieutenant Colonel)

**Field Officer:**  William R. Mitchell (Major)

**Assignments:**  5th Military District, Department of Mississippi and East Louisiana (April-May 1863)

Slemons' Brigade, 5th Military District, Department of Mississippi and East Louisiana (May-September 1863)

Chalmers' Cavalry Brigade, Department of Mississippi and East Louisiana (September-October 1863)

McCulloch's Brigade, Chalmers' Division, Lee's Cavalry Corps, Department of Mississippi and East Louisiana (October-December 1863)

Slemons' Brigade, Chalmers' Division, Lee's Cavalry Corps, Department of Mississippi and East Louisiana (December 1863-January 1864)

McCulloch's Brigade, Chalmers' Division, Lee's Cavalry Corps, Department of Mississippi and East Louisiana (January 1864)

McCulloch's Brigade, Chalmers' Division, Lee's Cavalry Corps, Department of Alabama, Mississippi, and East Louisiana (January-March 1864)

McCulloch's Brigade, Chalmers' Division, Forrest's Cavalry Corps, Department of Alabama, Mississippi, and East Louisiana (March-June 1864)

Unattached, Chalmers' Division, Forrest's Cavalry Corps, Department of Alabama, Mississippi, and East Louisiana (June 1864)

Rucker's Brigade, Chalmers' Division, Forrest's Cavalry Corps, Department of Alabama, Mississippi, and East Louisiana (June-July 1864)

Wade's-McCulloch's Brigade, Chalmers' Division, Forrest's Cavalry Corps, Department of Alabama, Mississippi, and East Louisiana (July-September 1864)

McCulloch's Cavalry Brigade, District of the Gulf, Department of Alabama, Mississippi, and East Louisiana (September-October 1864)

McCulloch's Cavalry Brigade, Liddell's Division, District of the Gulf, Department of Alabama, Mississippi, and East Louisiana (October-November 1864)

McCulloch's Cavalry Brigade, District of the Gulf, Department of Alabama, Mississippi, and East Louisiana (November-December 1864)

***Battles:***   Coldwater River [skirmish] (May 11, 1863)

Operations along the Memphis and Charleston Railroad (May 19-July 4, 1863)

Chalmers' Raid in West Tennessee and North Mississippi (October 4-17, 1863)

Colliersville (November 3, 1863)

Sturgis' Mississippi Expedition (June 1-13, 1864)

Brice's Crossroads (June 10, 1864)

Tupelo (July 14, 1864)

Forrest's Memphis Raid (August 21, 1864)

A.J. Smith's 2nd Mississippi Invasion (August 1864)

## 86.  MISSISSIPPI 18TH CAVALRY REGIMENT

***Also Known As:***   Chalmers' Consolidated Cavalry Regiment

***Organization:***   Organized ca. January 1865.  Field consolidation with five companies of the 5th Cavalry Regiment from February 18, 1865 to May 4, 1865. Surrendered by Lieutenant General Richard Taylor, commanding the Department of Alabama, Mississippi, and East Louisiana, at Meridian, Mississippi on May 4, 1865.

***First Commander:***   Alexander H. Chalmers (Colonel)

***Field Officers:***   James W. Smith (Lieutenant Colonel)

William J. Floyd (Major)

***Assignment:***   Starke's Brigade, Chalmers' Division, Forrest's Cavalry Corps, Department of Alabama, Mississippi, and East Louisiana (February-May 1865)

*Battle:*   Wilson's Raid (March-April 1865)

## 87.   MISSISSIPPI 19TH (DUFF'S) CAVALRY BATTALION

*Organization:*   Organized with six companies in the fall of 1863.  Increased to a regiment and designated as the 8th Cavalry Regiment in May 1864.

*First Commander:*   William L. Duff (Lieutenant Colonel)

*Field Officer:*   William L. Walker (Major)

*Assignments:*   Slemons' Brigade, Chalmers' Division, Lee's Cavalry Corps, Department of Mississippi and East Louisiana (October-November 1863)

McCulloch's Brigade, Chalmers' Division, Lee's Cavalry Corps, Department of Mississippi and East Louisiana (December 1863-January 1864)

McCulloch's Brigade, Chalmers' Division, Lee's Cavalry Corps, Department of Alabama, Mississippi, and East Louisiana (January-March 1864)

McCulloch's Brigade, Chalmers' Division, Forrest's Cavalry Corps, Department of Alabama, Mississippi, and East Louisiana (March-May 1864)

## 88.   MISSISSIPPI 19TH (GEORGE'S) CAVALRY BATTALION, STATE TROOPS

*Organization:*   Organized in the fall of 1863.  Increased to a regiment and designated as the 5th Cavalry Regiment in the fall of 1863.

*First Commander:*   James Z. George (Lieutenant Colonel)

*Field Officer:*   James A. Barksdale (Major)

*Assignment:*   Chalmers' Cavalry Brigade, Department of Mississippi and East Louisiana (September 1863)

## 89.   MISSISSIPPI 23RD CAVALRY BATTALION

*Organization:*   Organized by the assignment of the three Mississippi companies of Powers' Confederate Cavalry Regiment on November 21, 1864, per S.O. #276, Adjutant and Inspector General's Office.  Merged into Powers' (new Mississippi) Cavalry Regiment ca. March 3, 1865.

*First Commander:*   Joseph S. Terry (Major)

*Assignments:*   Sub-district of Southwest Mississippi and East Louisiana, District of Mississippi and East Louisiana, Department of Alabama, Mississippi, and East Louisiana (November 1864-February 1865)

Sub-district of South Mississippi, District of Mississippi and East Louisiana, Department of Alabama, Mississippi, and East Louisiana (February 1865)

W. Adams' Brigade, Chalmers' Division, Forrest's Cavalry Corps, Department of Alabama, Mississippi, and East Louisiana (February-March 1865)

## 90. MISSISSIPPI 24TH CAVALRY BATTALION

*Organization:* Organized with six companies from Moorman's Cavalry Battalion on January 24, 1865, per S.O. #19, Adjutant and Inspector General's Office. Surrendered by Lieutenant General Richard Taylor, commanding the Department of Alabama, Mississippi, and East Louisiana, at Meridian, Mississippi on May 4, 1865.

*First Commander:* William A. Pearcy (Lieutenant Colonel)

*Field Officer:* Calvit Roberts (Major)

*Assignment:* W. Adams' Brigade, Chalmers' Division, Forrest's Cavalry Corps, Department of Alabama, Mississippi, and East Louisiana (February-April 1865)

*Battles:* Wilson's Raid (March-April 1865)
Selma (April 2, 1865)

## 91. MISSISSIPPI 28TH CAVALRY REGIMENT

*Organization:* Organized ca. February 24, 1862. Field consolidation with part of the 7th Cavalry Regiment on February 18, 1865. Consolidated with the 3rd Cavalry Regiment and part of the 14th Confederate Cavalry Regiment and designated as the 3rd, 14th (Confederate), and 28th Cavalry Regiment Consolidated in February 1865.

*First Commander:* Peter B. Starke (Colonel)

*Field Officers:* Samuel W. Ferguson (Lieutenant Colonel)

Edward P. Jones (Major, Lieutenant Colonel)

Joshua T. McBee (Major)

*Assignments:* Department #1 (June 1862)

2nd/3rd Sub-district, District of the Mississippi, Department #2 (June-October 1862)

Department of Mississippi and East Louisiana (October 1862)

2nd Military District, Department of Mississippi and East Louisiana (October-December 1862)

1st Brigade, Jackson's Division, Jackson's-Van Dorn's Cavalry Corps, Army of North Mississippi, Department of Mississippi and East Louisiana (December 1862-February 1863)

Unattached, 2nd Military District, Department of Mississippi and East Louisiana [Company I] (December 1862-January 1863)

Lee's Command, 2nd Military District, Department of Mississippi and East Louisiana [Company I] (January 1863)

Cosby's Brigade, Martin's Division, Van Dorn's Cavalry Corps, Department of Mississippi and East Louisiana (February 1863)

Cosby's Brigade, Martin's Division, Van Dorn's Cavalry Corps, Army of Tennessee (March 1863)

Cosby's Brigade, Jackson's Cavalry Division, Department of Mississippi and East Louisiana (May-June 1863)

Cosby's Brigade, Jackson's Cavalry Division, Department of the West (June-July 1863)

Cosby's Brigade, Jackson's Cavalry Division, Department of Mississippi and East Louisiana (July-August 1863)

Cosby's Brigade, Jackson's Division, Lee's Cavalry Corps, Department of Mississippi and East Louisiana (August 1863-January 1864)

Cosby's-Starke's Brigade, Jackson's Division, Lee's Cavalry Corps, Department of Alabama, Mississippi, and East Louisiana (January-May 1864)

Starke's-Armstrong's Brigade, Jackson's Cavalry Division, Army of Mississippi (May-July 1864)

Armstrong's Brigade, Jackson's Cavalry Division, Army of Tennessee (July-November 1864)

Armstrong's Brigade, Jackson's Division, Forrest's Cavalry Corps, Army of Tennessee (November 1864-January 1865)

Armstrong's Brigade, Jackson's Division, Forrest's Cavalry Corps, Department of Alabama, Mississippi, and East Louisiana (January-February 1865)

Starke's Brigade, Chalmers' Division, Forrest's Cavalry Corps, Department of Alabama, Mississippi, and East Louisiana (February-May 1865)

**Battles:**  Vicksburg Bombardments (May 18-July 27, 1862)

Thompson's Station (March 5, 1863)

Vicksburg Campaign (May-July 1863)

Jones' Plantation, near Birdsong Ferry (June 22, 1863)

Jackson Siege (July 1863)

Meridian Campaign (February-March 1864)

Atlanta Campaign (May-September 1864)

Atlanta Siege (July-September 1864)

Campbellton (July 28, 1864)

Franklin (November 30, 1864)

Wilson's Raid (March-April 1865)

## 92.  MISSISSIPPI 38TH CAVALRY REGIMENT

*See:* MISSISSIPPI 38TH INFANTRY REGIMENT

## 93.  MISSISSIPPI 42ND CAVALRY REGIMENT

*See:* MISSISSIPPI 2ND CAVALRY REGIMENT

## 94.  MISSISSIPPI ADAMS', W.-WOOD'S CAVALRY REGIMENT

*Also Known As:*  1st Cavalry Regiment

W. Adams' Confederate Cavalry Regiment

Wood's Confederate Cavalry Regiment

**Organization:** Organized for the war on October 15, 1861. 1st Company G became independent in April 1862. Company N became 2nd Company G sometime after April 1862. 1st Company A became an independent unit in April 1862. Companies C, 1st D, and 1st M, were detached on May 16, 1862 and became Companies A, E, and B, respectively, 3rd Alabama Cavalry Regiment on July 1, 1862. 2nd Company M was organized on May 3, 1862 and was subsequently assigned to this regiment. 1st Company A became Company A, 15th Louisiana Cavalry Battalion on September 26, 1862. 2nd Company A was organized from a part of Company K on May 1, 1864. Surrendered by Lieutenant Richard Taylor, commanding the Department of Alabama, Mississippi, and East Louisiana, at Citronelle, Alabama on May 4, 1865.

**First Commander:** [William] Wirt Adams (Colonel)

**Field Officers:** Stephen B. Cleveland (Major)

James Hagan (Major)

Isaac F. Harrison (Major)

Thomas Lewers (Major, Lieutenant Colonel)

Robert C. Wood, Jr. (Lieutenant Colonel, Colonel)

**Assignments:** Cavalry, Hardee's Division, Central Army of Kentucky, Department #2 (October 1861-March 1862)

Beall's Cavalry Brigade, Department #2 (April-May 1862)

Beall's Cavalry Brigade, Department #2 (May-July 1862)

Armstrong's Cavalry Brigade, Price's Corps, Army of West Tennessee, Department #2 (July-October 1862)

Armstrong's Cavalry Brigade, Price's Corps, Army of West Tennessee, Department of Mississippi and East Louisiana (October 1862)

Unattached, 2nd Military District, Department of Mississippi and East Louisiana (December 1862-January 1863)

Unattached, Smith's Division, 2nd Military District, Department of Mississippi and East Louisiana (January-February 1863)

Unattached, Maury's Division, 2nd Military District, Department of Mississippi and East Louisiana (April 1863)

Unattached, Department of Mississippi and East Louisiana (April-June 1863)

J. Adams' Brigade, Walker's Division, Department of the West (June 1863)

Cosby's Brigade, Jackson's Cavalry Division, Department of the West (June-July 1863)

Cosby's-Jackson's-Cosby's Brigade, Jackson's Cavalry Division, Department of Mississippi and East Louisiana (July-August 1863)

Cosby's Brigade, Jackson's Division, Lee's Cavalry Corps, Department of Mississippi and East Louisiana (August-December 1863)

W. Adams' Brigade, Jackson's Division, Lee's Cavalry Corps, Department of
    Mississippi and East Louisiana (December 1863-January 1864)
W. Adams' Brigade, Jackson's Division, Lee's Cavalry Corps, Department of
    Alabama, Mississippi, and East Louisiana (January-May 1864)
Mabry's Brigade, W. Adams' Cavalry Division, Department of Alabama, Mis-
    sissippi, and East Louisiana (May-June 1864)
Wood's Brigade, W. Adams' Cavalry Division, Department of Alabama, Mis-
    sissippi, and East Louisiana (June-August 1864)
Wood's Brigade, District North of the Homochitto, Department of Alabama,
    Mississippi, and East Louisiana (August-October 1864)
Central Sub-district, District of Mississippi and East Louisiana, Department of
    Alabama, Mississippi, and East Louisiana (October 1864-February 1865)
W. Adams' Brigade, Chalmers' Division, Forrest's Cavalry Corps, Department
    of Alabama, Mississippi, and East Louisiana (February-May 1865)
**Battles:**   Woodbury [detachment] (October 29, 1861)
Morgantown [detachment] (October 31, 1861)
Scout in the vicinity of Russellville [detachment] (December 5-8, 1861)
Reconnaissance from Shiloh Battlefield [detachment] (April 8, 1862)
Corinth Campaign (April-June 1862)
Iuka (September 19, 1862)
Corinth (October 3-4, 1862)
Central Mississippi Campaign (October 1862-January 1863)
Grierson's Raid (April 17-May 2, 1863)
Union Church [skirmish] [three companies] (April 28, 1863)
Vicksburg Campaign (May-July 1863)
Raymond (May 12, 1863)
Big Black River Bridge [detachment] (May 17, 1863)
Yazoo River (May 23-31, 1863)
Jones' Plantation, near Birdsong Ferry (June 22, 1863)
Meridian Campaign (February-March 1864)
Concord Church (December 1, 1864)
Wilson's Raid (March-April 1865)

## 95. MISSISSIPPI ASHCRAFT'S CAVALRY REGIMENT

*Organization:*   Organized probably by the consolidation of the 3rd Cavalry
Battalion, the 3rd Cavalry Battalion, State Troops, and the 2nd Cavalry
Battalion, State Troops in the spring of 1864.  Consolidated with the 2nd
Cavalry Regiment, State Troops and Ham's Cavalry Regiment and designated
as Ashcraft's, Ham's and Lowry's Cavalry Regiment Consolidated on March
20, 1865.
*First Commander:*   Thomas C. Ashcraft (Colonel)

*Field Officers:*  E. L. Hankins (Major)

Thomas W. Harris (Lieutenant Colonel)

*Assignments:*  Gholson's Brigade, Forrest's Cavalry Corps, Department of Alabama, Mississippi, and East Louisiana (May 1864)

Gholson's Brigade, Buford's Division, Forrest's Cavalry Corps, Department of Alabama, Mississippi, and East Louisiana (May-June 1864)

Gholson's Brigade, W. Adams' Cavalry Division, Lee's Cavalry Corps, Department of Alabama, Mississippi, and East Louisiana (June-August 1864)

Armstrong's Brigade, Chalmers' Division, Forrest's Cavalry Corps, Department of Alabama, Mississippi, and East Louisiana (February-March 1865)

## 96.  MISSISSIPPI ASHCRAFT'S, HAM'S, AND LOWRY'S CAVALRY REGIMENT, CONSOLIDATED

*Organization:*  Organized by the consolidated of the 2nd Cavalry Regiment, State Troops and Ashcraft's and Ham's Cavalry Regiments on March 20, 1865. Surrendered by Lieutenant Richard Taylor, commanding the Department of Alabama, Mississippi, and East Louisiana, at Meridian, Mississippi on May 4, 1865.

*First Commander:*  Thomas C. Ashcraft (Colonel)

*Field Officers:*  William P. Curlee (Lieutenant Colonel)

L. L. Marshall (Major)

*Assignment:*  Armstrong's Brigade, Chalmers' Division, Forrest's Cavalry Corps, Department of Alabama, Mississippi, and East Louisiana (March-May 1865)

*Battles:*  Wilson's Raid (March-April 1865)

Selma (April 2, 1865)

## 97.  MISSISSIPPI BALLANTINE'S CAVALRY REGIMENT

*See:* MISSISSIPPI 2ND CAVALRY REGIMENT, PARTISAN RANGERS

## 98.  MISSISSIPPI BAXTER'S CAVALRY BATTALION

*See:* CONFEDERATE BAXTER'S CAVALRY BATTALION

## 99.  MISSISSIPPI BRADFORD'S SCOUTS CAVALRY BATTALION

*Organization:*  Organized with four companies in the fall of 1864. Its purpose was to facilitate communications across the Mississippi River with the Trans-Mississippi Department. Surrendered by Lieutenant General Richard Taylor, commanding the Department of Alabama, Mississippi, and East Louisiana, at Meridian, Mississippi on May 4, 1865.

*First Commander:*  J. D. Bradford (Major)

*Assignment:*  Griffith's Cavalry Brigade, Department of Alabama, Mississippi, and East Louisiana (November 1864-January 1865)
*Battle:*  Concord Church (December 1, 1864)

## 100.  MISSISSIPPI DAVENPORT'S CAVALRY BATTALION, STATE TROOPS

*Organization:*  Organized with three companies in the fall of 1863. Transferred to Confederate service in the fall of 1863. Apparently disbanded in early 1864.
*First Commander:*  Stephen Davenport (Major)
*Assignment:*  Richardson's Brigade, Chalmers' Cavalry Division, Department of Mississippi and East Louisiana (October-November 1863)

## 101.  MISSISSIPPI DUNN'S CAVALRY BATTALION, STATE TROOPS

*Organization:*  Organized for six months in early 1863. Mustered out in mid-1863.
*First Commander:*  John B. Dunn (Major)
*Assignment:*  5th Military District, Department of Mississippi and East Louisiana (April-May 1863)

## 102.  MISSISSIPPI GAMBLIN'S CAVALRY BATTALION, STATE TROOPS

*Organization:*  Organized in the summer of 1864. Apparently disbanded later in the year.
*First Commander:*  E. D. Gamblin (Captain)
*Assignment:*  Mabry's Cavalry Brigade, District North of Homochitto [W. Adams'], Department of Alabama, Mississippi, and East Louisiana (September-October 1864)

## 103.  MISSISSIPPI GARLAND'S CAVALRY BATTALION

*See:* MISSISSIPPI 14TH CAVALRY BATTALION, PARTISAN RANGERS

## 104.  MISSISSIPPI GORDON'S CAVALRY BATTALION

*Organization:*  Organized in 1862. Increased to a regiment and designated as the 2nd Cavalry Regiment later in 1862.
*First Commander:*  James Gordon (Lieutenant Colonel)

## 105.  MISSISSIPPI HAM'S CAVALRY BATTALION, STATE TROOPS

*See:* MISSISSIPPI 16TH CAVALRY BATTALION, STATE TROOPS

## 106.  MISSISSIPPI HAM'S CAVALRY REGIMENT

*Organization:*  Organized by the increase of the 16th Cavalry Battalion, State Troops to a regiment and is designated as Ham's Cavalry Regiment on April 30, 1864. Transferred to Confederate service on April 30, 1864. Consolidated with the 2nd Cavalry Regiment, State Troops and Ashcraft's Cavalry Regiment and designated as Ashcraft's, Ham's, and Lowry's Cavalry Regiment on March 20, 1865.

*First Commander:*  Thomas W. Ham (Colonel)

*Field Officers:*  George W. Bynum (Major)

William P. Curlee (Lieutenant Colonel)

*Assignments:*  Gholson's Brigade, Forrest's Cavalry Corps, Department of Alabama, Mississippi, and East Louisiana (May 1864)

Gholson's Brigade, Buford's Division, Forrest's Cavalry Corps, Department of Alabama, Mississippi, and East Louisiana (May-June 1864)

Gholson's Brigade, W. Adams' Cavalry Division, Lee's Cavalry Corps, Department of Alabama, Mississippi, and East Louisiana (June-August 1864)

Armstrong's Brigade, Chalmers' Division, Forrest's Cavalry Corps, Department of Alabama, Mississippi, and East Louisiana (February-March 1865)

## 107.  MISSISSIPPI HARRIS' CAVALRY BATTALION, STATE TROOPS

*See:* MISSISSIPPI 2ND CAVALRY BATTALION, STATE TROOPS

## 108.  MISSISSIPPI HUGHES' CAVALRY BATTALION, PARTISAN RANGERS

*Organization:*  Organized in early 1862. Consolidated with Stockdale's Cavalry Battalion and designated as the 4th Cavalry Regiment in November 1863.

*First Commander:*  Christopher C. Hughes (Major)

*Field Officer:*  Christopher C. Wilbourn (Lieutenant Colonel)

*Assignments:*  Port Hudson, Department #1 (April-June 1862)

Port Hudson, Department of Southern Mississippi and East Louisiana (June-July 1862)

1st Sub-district, District of the Mississippi, Department #2 (July-October 1862)

Department of Mississippi and East Louisiana (October 1862)

Cavalry, 3rd Military District, Department of Mississippi and East Louisiana (October 1862-September 1863)

Logan's Cavalry Command, Department of Mississippi and East Louisiana (September-November 1863)

Logan's-Griffith's Brigade, Jackson's Division, Lee's Cavalry Corps, Department of Mississippi and East Louisiana (November 1863)

*Battles:*  Grierson's Raid (April 17-May 2, 1863)

Port Hudson Siege (May-July 1863)

## 109. MISSISSIPPI JEFF. DAVIS CAVALRY LEGION

**Organization:**   Organized as the 2nd Mississippi Cavalry Battalion with three Mississippi and one Alabama companies on October 24, 1861. Increased to three Mississippi, one Georgia, and two Alabama companies and designated as the Jeff. Davis Legion in late 1861. Increased to a regiment by the addition of the three companies of the 4th Alabama Cavalry Battalion and Company D, 20th Georgia Cavalry Battalion on July 11, 1864. Surrendered by General Joseph E. Johnston at Durham Station, Orange County, North Carolina on April 26, 1865.

**First Commander:**   William T. Martin (Major, Lieutenant Colonel, Colonel)

**Field Officers:**   Richard M. Avery (Major)

William G. Conner (Major)

William G. Henderson (Major)

Ivey F. Lewis (Major)

William M. Stone (Major)

Joseph F. Waring (Lieutenant Colonel, Colonel)

**Assignments:**   Cavalry Brigade, Potomac District, Department of Northern Virginia (December 1861-March 1862)

Cavalry Brigade, Army of Northern Virginia (March-July 1862)

Hampton's Brigade, Cavalry Division, Army of Northern Virginia (July 1862-September 1863)

Butler's-Young's Brigade, Hampton's-Butler's Division, Cavalry Corps, Army of Northern Virginia (September 1863-January 1865)

Young's Brigade, Butler's Division, Hampton's Cavalry Command (January-April 1865)

Logan's Brigade, Butler's Division, Hampton's Cavalry Command, Army of Tennessee (April 1865)

**Battles:**   Doolan's Farm (November 16, 1861)

Yorktown Siege (April-May 1862)

Williamsburg [skirmish] (May 4, 1862)

Williamsburg (May 5, 1862)

Stuart's First Ride Around McClellan (June 13-15, 1862)

Seven Days Battles (June 25-July 1, 1862)

Reconnaissance toward Forge Bridge (August 17, 1862)

Catoctin Mountain (September 13, 1862)

Antietam (September 17, 1862)

near Hartwood Church [skirmish] [detachment] (November 28, 1862)

Dumfries [detachment] (December 12, 1862)

on the Occoquan River [skirmish] (December 19, 1862)

Brandy Station (June 9, 1863)
Upperville (June 21, 1863)
Gettysburg (July 1-3, 1863)
Bristoe Campaign (October 1863)
Mine Run Campaign (November-December 1863)
The Wilderness (May 5-6, 1864)
Spotsylvania Court House (May 8-21, 1864)
North Anna (May 23-26, 1864)
Cold Harbor (June 1-3, 1864)
Petersburg Siege (June 1864-April 1865)
Williamsburg Road (October 27, 1864)
Carolinas Campaign (February-April 1865)

## 110. MISSISSIPPI LAY'S CAVALRY REGIMENT

*See:* CONFEDERATE 20TH CAVALRY REGIMENT

## 111. MISSISSIPPI LINDSAY'S IMPROVISED CAVALRY REGIMENT

*Also Known As:* 1st Mississippi Cavalry Regiment

*Organization:* Organized with nine companies by the consolidation of the 1st (Miller's) Mississippi Cavalry Battalion and independent companies on April 2, 1862. Broken up in the spring of 1862.

*First Commander:* Andrew J. Lindsay (Colonel)

*Field Officer:* John H. Miller (Lieutenant Colonel)

*Assignments:* Cavalry Reserve, Army of the Mississippi, Department #2 (April 1862)

Cavalry, 1st Corps, Army of the Mississippi, Department #2 (April 1862)

Beall's Cavalry Brigade, Department #2 (April-May 1862)

*Battles:* Shiloh (April 6-7, 1862)

Corinth Campaign (April-June 1862)

Farron's Mill [skirmish] (May 5, 1862)

## 112. MISSISSIPPI MCLAURIN'S CAVALRY BATTALION

*Organization:* Organized in the spring of 1863. Disbanded later in the spring of 1863.

*First Commander:* Cornelius McLaurin (Major)

*Assignment:* Ponchatoula, 3rd Military District, Department of Mississippi and East Louisiana (April-May 1863)

## 113.  MISSISSIPPI MATTHEWS' CAVALRY BATTALION, STATE TROOPS

**Organization:**  Organized for six months in early 1863. Mustered out in mid-1863.

**First Commander:**  Samuel Matthews (Captain)

**Assignment:**  5th Military District, Department of Mississippi and East Louisiana (March-May 1863)

## 114.  MISSISSIPPI MONTGOMERY'S CAVALRY BATTALION, RESERVES

**Organization:**  Organized with four companies in the summer of 1864. Surrendered by Lieutenant General Richard Taylor, commanding the Department of Alabama, Mississippi, and East Louisiana, at Meridian, Mississippi on May 4, 1865.

**First Commander:**  William E. Montgomery (Major)

**Assignments:**  Wood's Cavalry Brigade, District North of Homochitto [Wirt Adams' command] (September-October 1864)

Griffith's Cavalry Brigade, Department of Alabama, Mississippi, and East Louisiana (October-November 1864)

**Battles:**  Expedition to Yazoo City (November 23-December 4, 1864)

Concord Church (December 1, 1864)

## 115.  MISSISSIPPI MOORMAN'S CAVALRY BATTALION

**Organization:**  Organized with four companies in early 1864. Redesignated as the 24th Cavalry Battalion on January 24, 1865, per S.O. #19, Adjutant and Inspector General's Office.

**First Commander:**  George Moorman (Lieutenant Colonel)

**Field Officer:**  Calvit Roberts (Major)

**Assignments:**  W. Adams' Brigade, Jackson's Division, Lee's Cavalry Corps, Department of Alabama, Mississippi, and East Louisiana (April 1864)

Mabry's Brigade, W. Adams' Cavalry Division, Department of Alabama, Mississippi, and East Louisiana (May-June 1864)

Wood's Brigade, W. Adams' Cavalry Division, Department of Alabama, Mississippi, and East Louisiana (June-August 1864)

Wood's Cavalry Brigade, District North of Homochitto [W. Adams' command], District of Mississippi and East Louisiana, Department of Alabama, Mississippi, and East Louisiana (August-October 1864)

Denis' Brigade, Northern Sub-district, District of Mississippi & East Louisiana, Department of Alabama, Mississippi, and East Louisiana (November 1864-January 1865)

## 116. MISSISSIPPI PERRIN'S CAVALRY BATTALION, STATE TROOPS

*Organization:* Organized with nine companies in 1863. Transferred to Confederate service on September 11, 1863. Increased to a regiment and designated as the 11th Cavalry Regiment in early 1864.

*First Commander:* Robert O. Perrin (Lieutenant Colonel)

*Field Officer:* Absalom C. Reed (Major)


## 117. MISSISSIPPI PEYTON'S CAVALRY BATTALION, RESERVES

*Organization:* Organized the summer of 1864. Surrendered by Lieutenant General Richard Taylor, commanding the Department of Alabama, Mississippi, and East Louisiana, at Meridian, Mississippi on May 4, 1865.

*First Commander:* E. A. Peyton (Major)

*Assignments:* Wood's Brigade, W. Adams' Cavalry Division, Department of Alabama, Mississippi, and East Louisiana (July-August 1864)

Wood's Cavalry Brigade, District North of Homochitto [W. Adams' command], Department of Alabama, Mississippi, and East Louisiana (August-October 1864)

Central Sub-district, District of Mississippi and East Louisiana, Department of Alabama, Mississippi, and East Louisiana (November 1864-May 1865)


## 118. MISSISSIPPI [AND LOUISIANA] POWERS' CAVALRY REGIMENT

*See:* CONFEDERATE POWERS' CAVALRY REGIMENT


## 119. MISSISSIPPI POWERS' (NEW) CAVALRY REGIMENT

*Organization:* Organized in part from the 23rd Cavalry Battalion ca. March 3, 1865. Surrendered by Lieutenant General Richard Taylor, commanding the Department of Alabama, Mississippi, and East Louisiana, at Meridian, Mississippi on May 4, 1865.

*First Commander:* Frank P. Powers (Colonel)

*Assignment:* W. Adams' Brigade, Chalmers' Division, Forrest's Cavalry Corps, Department of Alabama, Mississippi, and East Louisiana (March-May 1865)

*Battle:* Wilson's Raid (March-April 1865)


## 120. MISSISSIPPI SMITH'S CAVALRY REGIMENT, STATE TROOPS

*See:* MISSISSIPPI 2ND CAVALRY REGIMENT, STATE TROOPS

### 121.  MISSISSIPPI SMYTH'S CAVALRY BATTALION

*Organization:*  Organized in late 1863.  Apparently a temporary organization of those cavalry units captured and paroled at Vicksburg, Warren County, Mississippi.  Broken up in early 1864.

*First Commander:*   J. S. Smyth (Major [acting])

*Assignments:*  Beltzhoover's Brigade, Forney's Command, Department of Mississippi and East Louisiana (December 1863-January 1864)

Beltzhoover's Brigade, Forney's Command, Department of Alabama, Mississippi, and East Louisiana (January 1864)

### 122.  MISSISSIPPI STOCKDALE'S CAVALRY BATTALION

*Organization:*  Organized in the spring of 1863.  Consolidated with Hughes' Cavalry Battalion, Partisan Rangers and designated as the 4th Mississippi Cavalry Regiment in November 1863.

*First Commander:*  Thomas R. Stockdale (Major)

*Assignments:*  Cavalry, 3rd Military District, Department of Mississippi and East Louisiana (June-September 1863)

Logan's Cavalry Command, Department of Mississippi and East Louisiana (September-November 1863)

Logan's-Griffith's Brigade, Jackson's Division, Lee's Cavalry Corps, Department of Mississippi and East Louisiana (November 1863)

*Battle:*   Port Hudson Siege (May-July 1863)

### 123.  MISSISSIPPI STREET'S CAVALRY BATTALION

*Organization:*  Organized in late 1863.  Apparently broken up in early 1864.

*First Commander:*   Solomon G. Street (Major)

*Assignments:*  Richardson's Brigade, Forrest's Cavalry Corps, Department of Mississippi and East Louisiana (January 1864)

Richardson's Brigade, Forrest's Cavalry Corps, Department of Alabama, Mississippi, and East Louisiana (January-February 1864)

### 124.  MISSISSIPPI STUBBS' CAVALRY BATTALION, RESERVES

*Organization:*  Organized in the summer 1864.  Surrendered by Lieutenant General Richard Taylor, commanding the Department of Alabama, Mississippi, and East Louisiana, at Meridian, Mississippi on May 4, 1865.

*First Commander:*  George W. Stubbs (Major)

*Assignments:*  Wood's Brigade, W. Adams' Cavalry Division, Department of Alabama, Mississippi, and East Louisiana (July-August 1864)

Wood's Cavalry Brigade, District North of Homochitto [W. Adams' command], Department of Alabama, Mississippi, and East Louisiana (August-November 1864)

Griffith's Cavalry Brigade, Department of Alabama, Mississippi, and East Louisiana (November 1864)

Central Sub-district, District of Mississippi and East Louisiana, Department of Alabama, Mississippi, and East Louisiana (November 1864-May 1865)

**Battles:** Expedition to Yazoo City (November 23-December 4, 1864)

Concord Church (December 1, 1864)

# INFANTRY

## 125. MISSISSIPPI 1ST (BLYTHE'S) INFANTRY BATTALION

**Organization:** Organized in the summer of 1861. Increased to a regiment and designated as Blythe's Infantry Regiment in the fall of 1861.

**First Commander:** Andrew K. Blythe (Major, Lieutenant Colonel)

**Assignments:** 1st (Cheatham's) Brigade, 1st Geographical Division, Department #2 (September-October 1861)

1st (Smith's) Brigade, 2nd (Cheatham's) Division, 1st Geographical Division, Department #2 (October 1861)

## 126. MISSISSIPPI 1ST (CHOCTAW) INFANTRY BATTALION

**Organization:** Organized in early 1863. Apparently disbanded in the summer of 1863.

**First Commander:** J. W. Pierce (Major)

**Assignment:** 4th Military District, Department of Mississippi and East Louisiana (February-May 1863)

**Battle:** Vicksburg Campaign (May-July 1863)

## 127. MISSISSIPPI 1ST INFANTRY BATTALION, SHARPSHOOTERS

**Also Known As:** 10th Sharpshooters Battalion

20th Sharpshooters Battalion

**Organization:** Organized in May 1862. Companies A, B, and D were assigned from the 2nd Confederate Infantry Regiment. Consolidated with the 1st, 22nd, and 33rd Infantry Regiments and designated as the 22nd Infantry Regiment Consolidated at Smithfield, North Carolina on April 9, 1865.

**First Commander:** James M. Stigler (Major)

**Field Officer:** William A. Rayburn (Major)

**Assignments:** Rust's Brigade, Loring's Division, Army of North Mississippi, Department of Mississippi and East Louisiana (January-February 1863)

Featherston's Brigade, Loring's Division, 2nd Military District, Department of Mississippi and East Louisiana (March-April 1863)

Featherston's Brigade, Loring's Division, Department of Mississippi and East Louisiana (April-May 1863)

Featherston's Brigade, Loring's Division, Department of the West (May-July 1863)

Featherston's Brigade, Loring's Division, Department of Mississippi and East Louisiana (July 1863-January 1864)

Featherston's Brigade, Loring's Division, Department of Alabama, Mississippi, and East Louisiana (January-May 1864)

Featherston's Brigade, Loring's Division, Army of Mississippi (May-July 1864)

Featherston's Brigade, Loring's Division, 3rd Corps, Army of Tennessee (July 1864-April 1865)

**Battles:**  Vicksburg Campaign (May-July 1863)

Champion Hill (May 16, 1863)

Jackson Siege (July 1863)

Meridian Campaign (February-March 1864)

Atlanta Campaign (May-September 1864)

New Hope Church (May 25-June 4, 1864)

Peach Tree Creek (July 20, 1864)

Ezra Church (July 28, 1864)

Atlanta Siege (July-September 1864)

Jonesboro (August 31-September 1, 1864)

Franklin (November 30, 1864)

Nashville (December 15-16, 1864)

Carolinas Campaign (February-April 1865)

## 128.  MISSISSIPPI 1ST INFANTRY BATTALION, STATE TROOPS

*Also Known As:*  1st Infantry Battalion Minute Men

13th Infantry Battalion

*Organization:*  Organized for six months with five companies in the fall of 1862. Mounted in early 1863. Mustered out in the summer of 1863.

*First Commander:*  W. B. Harper (Major)

*Assignment:*  4th Military District, Department of Mississippi and East Louisiana (January-April 1863)

*Battles:*  Mouth of the Coldwater (November 28, 1862)

Vicksburg Campaign (May-July 1863)

Raymond (May 12, 1863)

Jackson (May 14, 1863)

## 129. MISSISSIPPI 1ST INFANTRY REGIMENT

*Organization:* Organized in 1861. Surrendered at Fort Donelson on February 16, 1862. Exchanged in late 1862. Field consolidation with the 1st Alabama, Tennessee, and Mississippi Infantry Regiment in late 1862. Field consolidation with the 39th Infantry Regiment in January 1863. Surrendered at Port Hudson on July 8, 1864. Paroled in July 1863. Exchanged ca. November 1863. Reorganized at Okolona November 1863. Consolidated with the 1st Sharpshooters Battalion and the 22nd and 33rd Infantry Regiments and designated as the 22nd Infantry Regiment Consolidated at Smithfield, North Carolina on April 9, 1865.

*First Commander:* John M. Simonton (Colonel)

*Field Officers:* Milton S. Alcorn (Major)

Alexander S. Hamilton (Lieutenant Colonel)

Thomas H. Johnston (Major, Colonel)

*Assignments:* Clark's Brigade, Central Army of Kentucky, Department #2 (December 1861-February 1862)

Davidson's Brigade, Johnson's Division, Fort Donelson, Department #2 (February 1862)

1st Brigade, Maury's Division, Price's Corps, Army of North Mississippi, Department of Mississippi and East Louisiana (October-December 1862)

Thompson's Brigade, Rust's Division, 2nd Corps, Army of North Mississippi, Department of Mississippi and East Louisiana (December 1862-January 1863)

Beall's Brigade, 3rd Military District, Department of Mississippi and East Louisiana (January-July 1863)

Unattached, Forney's Division, Department of Mississippi and East Louisiana (November 1863)

Featherston's Brigade, Loring's Division, Department of Alabama, Mississippi, and East Louisiana (February-May 1864)

Featherston's Brigade, Loring's Division, Army of Mississippi (May-July 1864)

Featherston's Brigade, Loring's Division, 3rd Corps, Army of Tennessee (July 1864-April 1865)

*Battles:* Fort Donelson (February 12-16, 1862)

Port Hudson Siege (May-July 1863)

Atlanta Campaign (May-September 1864)

Ezra Church (July 28, 1864)

New Hope Church (May 25-June 4, 1864)

Peach Tree Creek (July 20, 1864)

Jonesboro (August 31-September 1, 1864)

Atlanta Siege (July-September 1864)

Franklin (November 30, 1864)

Nashville (December 15-16, 1864)
Carolinas Campaign (February-April 1865)

## 130. MISSISSIPPI 1ST INFANTRY REGIMENT, MILITIA

**Organization:** Organized for six months at Grenada in Decmber 1861. Mustered out in mid-1862.
**First Commander:** William A. Percy (Colonel)
**Field Officers:** Wade Hopkins (Major)
Samuel M. Meek (Lieutenant Colonel)
**Assignment:** Alcorn's Brigade, Central Army of Kentucky, Department #2 (December 1861-January 1862)

## 131. MISSISSIPPI 1ST INFANTRY REGIMENT, STATE TROOPS

**Also Known As:** 1st Infantry Regiment, Minute Men
**Organization:** Organized for six months in late 1862. Mustered out in early 1863.
**First Commander:** Benjamin King (Colonel)
**Field Officers:** J. Lawhon (Lieutenant Colonel)
B. F. Sutton (Major)

## 132. MISSISSIPPI 1ST MISSISSIPPI VALLEY INFANTRY REGIMENT

**See:** CONFEDERATE 4TH INFANTRY REGIMENT

## 133. MISSISSIPPI 2ND INFANTRY BATTALION

**Organization:** Organized on October 16, 1861, per S.O. #181, Adjutant and Inspector General's Office. Increased to a regiment and designated as the 48th Infantry Regiment on January 17, 1863.
**First Commander:** John G. Taylor (Lieutenant Colonel)
**Field Officers:** Levi C. Lee (Major)
Thomas B. Manlove (Lieutenant Colonel)
William S. Wilson (Major, Lieutenant Colonel)
**Assignments:** Rains' Division, Department of the Peninsula (January-February 1862)
Ward's Command, Early's Division, D. H. Hill's Command, Department of Northern Virginia (March-May 1862)
Ward's Command, D. H. Hill's Division, Department of Northern Virginia (May 1862)
Garland's Brigade, D. H. Hill's Division, Army of Northern Virginia (May-June 1862)

Featherston's Brigade, Longstreet's Division, Army of Northern Virginia (June 1862)

Featherston's Brigade, Longstreet's Division, 1st Corps, Army of Northern Virginia (June-August 1862)

Featherston's Brigade, Wilcox's Division, 1st Corps, Army of Northern Virginia (August-September 1862)

Featherston's Brigade, R. H. Anderson's Division, 1st Corps, Army of Northern Virginia (September 1862-January 1863)

**Battles:** Yorktown Siege (April-May 1862)

Williamsburg (May 5, 1862)

Seven Pines (May 31-June 1, 1862)

Seven Days Battles (June 25-July 1, 1862)

Gaines' Mill (June 27, 1862)

Frayser's Farm (June 30, 1862)

2nd Bull Run (August 28-30, 1862)

Antietam (September 17, 1862)

Fredericksburg (December 13, 1862)

## 134. MISSISSIPPI 2ND INFANTRY BATTALION, STATE TROOPS

*Also Known As:* 2nd Infantry Battalion, Minute Men

*Organization:* Organized for six months with five companies in late 1862. Mustered out in early 1863.

*First Commander:* Henry F. Cook (Major)

*Assignment:* Hébert's Brigade, Maury's Division, 2nd Military District, Department of Mississippi and East Louisiana (January-April 1863)

## 135. MISSISSIPPI 2ND INFANTRY REGIMENT

*Organization:* Organized with 11 companies on May 10, 1861. Reorganized on April 16, 1862. Surrendered at Appomattox Court House, Virginia on April 9, 1865.

*First Commander:* William C. Falkner (Colonel)

*Field Officers:* John A. Blair (Major, Lieutenant Colonel)

Bartley B. Boone (Lieutenant Colonel)

John H. Buchanan (Major)

David W. Humphreys (Major, Lieutenant Colonel)

John M. Stone (Colonel)

*Assignments:* Harpers Ferry (May-June 1861)

Bee's Brigade, Army of the Shenandoah (June-July 1861)

Bee's-Whiting's Brigade, 2nd Corps, Army of the Potomac (July-October 1861)

Whiting's Brigade, Forces near Dumfries [Whiting's Command], 2nd Corps, Potomac District, Department of Northern Virginia (October 1861-March 1862)

Whiting's Brigade, Whiting's Division, Army of Northern Virginia (March-June 1862)

Whiting's Brigade, Whiting's Division, Valley District, Department of Northern Virginia (June 1862)

Whiting's Brigade, Whiting's Division, 2nd Corps, Army of Northern Virginia (June-July 1862)

Whiting's-Law's Brigade, Whiting's-Hood's Division, 1st Corps, Army of Northern Virginia (July-September 1862)

Davis' Brigade, Unattached, Department of North Carolina and Southern Virginia (December 1862)

Davis' Brigade, French's Command, Department of North Carolina and Southern Virginia (December 1862-February 1863)

Davis' Brigade, Department of Southern Virginia (May 1863)

Davis' Brigade, Department of North Carolina (May 1863)

Davis' Brigade, Heth's Division, 3rd Corps, Army of Northern Virginia (June 1863-April 1865)

**Battles:**   1st Bull Run (July 21, 1861)

Yorktown Siege (April-May 1862)

Seven Pines (May 31-June 1, 1862)

Seven Days Battles (June 25-July 1, 1862)

Gaines' Mill (June 27, 1862)

Malvern Hill (July 1, 1862)

2nd Bull Run (August 28-30, 1862)

South Mountain (September 14, 1862)

Antietam (September 17, 1862)

Gettysburg (July 1-3, 1863)

Falling Waters (July 14, 1863)

Bristoe Campaign (October 1863)

Mine Run Campaign (November-December 1863)

The Wilderness (May 5-6, 1864)

Spotsylvania Court House (May 8-21, 1864)

North Anna (May 23-26, 1864)

Cold Harbor (June 1-3, 1864)

Petersburg Siege (June 1864-April 1865)

Weldon Railroad (August 18-22, 1864)

Hatcher's Run (February 5-7, 1865)

Appomattox Court House (April 9, 1865)

**Further Reading:**   Hankins, Samuel W., *Simple Story of a Soldier.*

## 136.  MISSISSIPPI 2ND INFANTRY REGIMENT, MILITIA

*Organization:* Organized for six months at Grenada in December 1861. Mustered out in mid 1862.
*First Commander:* Bartlett (Colonel)
*Field Officer:* M. B. Buchanan (Lieutenant Colonel)
*Assignment:* Alcorn's Brigade, 1st Geographical Division, Western Department, Dept #2 (December 1861-January 1862)

## 137.  MISSISSIPPI 2ND INFANTRY REGIMENT, STATE TROOPS

*Organization:* Organized for six months in late 1862. Mustered out in mid-1863.
*First Commander:* D. H. Quinn (Colonel)
*Field Officers:* James M. Conerly (Lieutenant Colonel)
Jacob O. Magee (Major)
*Assignment:* Hébert's Brigade, Maury's Division, 2nd Military District, Department of Mississippi and East Louisiana (January-April 1863)

## 138.  MISSISSIPPI 2ND (DAVIDSON'S) INFANTRY REGIMENT

*See:* MISSISSIPPI 23RD INFANTRY REGIMENT

## 139.  MISSISSIPPI 3RD (HARDCASTLE'S) INFANTRY BATTALION

*Organization:* Organized at Grenada with three companies in late 1861. A fourth company was added in early 1862. Increased to a regiment and designated as the 33rd (Hardcastle's) Infantry Regiment in April 1862.
*First Commander:* Aaron B. Hardcastle (Major)
*Assignments:* 1st Geographical Division, Department #2 (December 1861)
Wood's Brigade, Hardee's Division, Central Army of Kentucky, Department #2 (December 1861-February 1862)
Wood's Brigade, Pillow's Division, 1st Geographical Division, Department #2 (February 1862)
Department #1 (March 1862)
Wood's Brigade, 3rd Corps, Army of the Mississippi, Department #2 (March-April 1862)
*Battle:* Shiloh (April 6-7, 1862)

## 140.  MISSISSIPPI 3RD (WILLIAMS') INFANTRY BATTALION

*Organization:* Organized by the reduction of the 45th Infantry Regiment to a battalion on July 24, 1864. Field consolidation with the 5th Infantry Regiment from July 24, 1864 to April 9, 1865. Consolidated with part of the 5th Infantry Regiment and the 8th and 32nd Infantry Regiments and designated as the 8th Infantry Battalion Consolidated at Smithfield, North Carolina on April 9, 1865.

**First Commander:**  John D. Williams (Lieutenant Colonel)

**Field Officer:**  Elisha F. Nunn (Major)

**Assignment:**  Lowrey's Brigade, Cleburne's Division, 1st Corps, Army of Tennessee (July 1864-April 1865)

**Battles:**  Atlanta Campaign (May-September 1864)

Jonesboro (August 31-September 1, 1864)

Atlanta Siege (July-September 1864)

Franklin (November 30, 1864)

Nashville (December 15-16, 1864)

Carolinas Campaign (February-April 1865)

Bentonville (March 19-21, 1865)

### 141.  MISSISSIPPI 3RD INFANTRY BATTALION, STATE TROOPS

**Also Known As:**  3rd Infantry Battalion, Minute Men

**Organization:**  Organized for six months with five companies in late 1862. Surrendered at Vicksburg, Warren County, Mississippi on July 4, 1863. Paroled at Vicksburg, Warren County, Mississippi on July 4, 1863. Apparently never reorganized.

**First Commander:**  Thomas A. Burgin (Lieutenant Colonel)

**Field Officer:**  Benjamin B. Moore (Major)

**Assignments:**  1st Military District, Department of Mississippi and East Louisiana (January-April 1863)

Harris' Brigade, Mississippi State Troops [attached to Vaughn's Brigade], Smith's Division, Department of Mississippi and East Louisiana (April-July 1863)

**Battles:**  Vicksburg Campaign (May-July 1863)

Vicksburg Siege (May-July 1863)

### 142.  MISSISSIPPI 3RD INFANTRY REGIMENT

**Organization:**  Organized in 1861.  Consolidated with the 31st and 40th Infantry Regiments and designated as the 3rd Infantry Regiment Consolidated at Smithfield, North Carolina on April 9, 1865.

**First Commander:**  John B. Deason (Colonel)

**Field Officers:**  Samuel M. Dyer (Major, Lieutenant Colonel)

Robert Eager (Lieutenant Colonel)

James B. McRae (Lieutenant Colonel)

Thomas A. Mellon (Major, Lieutenant Colonel, Colonel)

William H. Morgan (Major)

E. A. Peyton (Major)

**Assignments:** Department #1 (December 1861-January 1862)

Department of Southern Mississippi and East Louisiana (June-July 1862)

2nd Sub-district, District of the Mississippi, Department #2 (July-August 1862)

3rd Sub-district, District of the Mississippi, Department #2 (September-October 1862)

Department of Mississippi and East Louisiana (October 1862)

2nd Military District, Department of Mississippi and East Louisiana (October-December 1862)

Thomas' Brigade, Lee's-Maury's Provisional Division, 2nd Military District, Department of Mississippi and East Louisiana (December 1862-January 1863)

Lee's Command, 2nd Military District, Department of Mississippi and East Louisiana (January 1863)

Hébert's Brigade, Maury's Division, 2nd Military District, Department of Mississippi and East Louisiana (January-April 1863)

Featherston's Brigade, Loring's Division, Department of Mississippi and East Louisiana (April-May 1863)

Featherston's Brigade, Loring's Division, Department of the West (May-July 1863)

Featherston's Division, Loring's Division, Department of Mississippi and East Louisiana (July 1863-January 1864)

Featherston's Brigade, Loring's Division, Department of Alabama, Mississippi, and East Louisiana (January-May 1864)

Featherston's Brigade, Loring's Division, Army of Mississippi (May-July 1864)

Featherston's Brigade, Loring's Division, 3rd Corps, Army of Tennessee (July 1864-April 1865)

**Battles:** Biloxi [seven companies] (April 3, 1862)

Christian Pass [three companies] (April 4, 1862)

Vicksburg Bombardments (May 18-July 27, 1862)

Chickasaw Bayou (December 27-29, 1862)

Vicksburg Campaign (May-July 1863)

Champion Hill (May 16, 1863)

Jackson Siege (July 1863)

Meridian Campaign (February-March 1864)

Atlanta Campaign (May-September 1864)

New Hope Church (May 25-June 4, 1864)

Peach Tree Creek (July 20, 1864)

Ezra Church (July 28, 1864)

Atlanta Siege (July-September 1864)

Jonesboro (August 31-September 1, 1864)

Franklin (November 30, 1864)

Nashville (December 15-16, 1864)
Carolinas Campaign (February-April 1865)

### 143.  MISSISSIPPI 3RD INFANTRY REGIMENT, CONSOLIDATED

*Organization:* Organized by the consolidation of the 3rd, 31st, and 40th Infantry Regiments at Smithfield, North Carolina on April 9, 1865. Surrendered by General Joseph E. Johnston at Durham Station, Orange County, North Carolina on April 26, 1865.
*First Commander:* John M. Stigler (Colonel)
*Assignment:* Featherston's Brigade, Loring's Division, 3rd Corps, Army of Tennessee (April 1865)
*Battle:* Carolinas Campaign (February-April 1865)

### 144.  MISSISSIPPI 3RD INFANTRY REGIMENT, MILITIA

*Organization:* Organized for six months at Grenada on December 1861. Mustered out in mid-1862.
*First Commander:* B. L. Rozell (Colonel)
*Assignment:* Alcorn's Brigade, Central Army of Kentucky, Department #2 (December 1861-January 1862)

### 145.  MISSISSIPPI 3RD INFANTRY REGIMENT, STATE TROOPS

*Organization:* Organized for six months in late 1862. Mustered out in mid-1863.
*First Commander:* Winfrey J. Owens (Colonel)
*Field Officers:* J. A. Harlin (Lieutenant Colonel)
Fleet C. Mercer (Major)
*Assignments:* Thomas' Brigade, Lee's-Maury's Provisional Division, 2nd Military District, Department of Mississippi and East Louisiana (December 1862-January 1863)
Lee's Command, 2nd Military District, Department of Mississippi and East Louisiana (January 1863)
Lee's Brigade, Smith's Division, 2nd Military District, Department of Mississippi and East Louisiana (January 1863)
*Battle:* Chickasaw Bayou (December 27-29, 1862)

### 146.  MISSISSIPPI 4TH INFANTRY BATTALION, STATE TROOPS

*Also Known As:* 4th Infantry Battalion, Minute Men
*Organization:* Organized for six months with five companies in late 1862. Mustered out in mid-1863.
*First Commander:* A. J. Postlethwaite (Lieutenant Colonel)
*Field Officer:* John D. Farley (Major)

## 147.   MISSISSIPPI 4TH INFANTRY REGIMENT

*Organization:*   Organized in 1861. Surrendered at Fort Donelson on February 16, 1862. Declared exchanged on August 27, 1862. Regiment surrendered at Vicksburg, Warren County, Mississippi on July 4, 1863. Paroled at Vicksburg, Warren County, Mississippi in July 1863. Declared exchanged on September 12, 1863. Surrendered by Lieutenant Richard Taylor, commanding the Department of Alabama, Mississippi, and East Louisiana, at Citronelle, Alabama on May 4, 1865.

*First Commander:*   Joseph Drake (Colonel)

*Field Officers:*   Thomas N. Adaire (Major, Lieutenant Colonel, Colonel)
Joseph J. Gee (Major, Lieutenant Colonel)
Pierre S. Layton (Lieutenant Colonel, Colonel)
Thomas P. Nelson (Major)

*Assignments:*   Drake's Brigade, Fort Henry, Department #2 (February 1862)

Drake's Brigade, Johnson's Division, Fort Donelson, Department #2 (February 1862)

Department of Mississippi and East Louisiana (October 1862)

3rd Military District, Department of Mississippi and East Louisiana (October-December 1862)

Thomas' Brigade, Lee's-Maury's Provisional Division, 2nd Military District, Department of Mississippi and East Louisiana (December 1862-January 1863)

Lee's Command, 2nd Military District, Department of Mississippi and East Louisiana (January 1863)

Lee's Brigade, Smith's Division, 2nd Military District, Department of Mississippi and East Louisiana (January-February 1863)

Baldwin's Brigade, Smith's Division, 2nd Military District, Department of Mississippi and East Louisiana (April 1863)

Baldwin's Brigade, Smith's Division, Department of Mississippi and East Louisiana (April-July 1863)

Baldwin's Brigade, Walker's Division, 1st Corps, Army of Tennessee (December 1863-January 1864)

Baldwin's Brigade, Department of the Gulf (January-March 1864)

Baldwin's [old]-Sears' Brigade, Department of Alabama, Mississippi, and East Louisiana (March-May 1864)

Sears' Brigade, Army of Mississippi (May 1864)

Sears' Brigade, French's Division, Army of Mississippi (May-July 1864)

Sears' Brigade, French's Division, 3rd Corps, Army of Tennessee (July-December 1864)

Sears' Brigade, French's Division, District of the Gulf, Department of Alabama, Mississippi, and East Louisiana (March-April 1865)

Sears' Brigade, French's Division, Department of Alabama, Mississippi, and
East Louisiana (April-May 1865)

**Battles:**  Fort Henry (February 6, 1862)
Fort Donelson (February 12-16, 1862)
Chickasaw Bayou (December 27-29, 1862)
Vicksburg Campaign (May-July 1863)
Port Gibson (May 1, 1863)
Vicksburg Siege (May-July 1863)
Atlanta Campaign (May-September 1864)
Cassville (May 19-22, 1864)
New Hope Church (May 25-June 4, 1864)
Lattimer's Mills (June 20, 1864)
Kennesaw Mountain (June 27, 1864)
Atlanta Siege (July-September 1864)
Smyrna Campground (July 4, 1864)
Chattahoochee River (July 5-17, 1864)
Peach Tree Creek (July 20, 1864)
Ezra Church (July 28, 1864)
Atlanta (July 22, 1864)
Jonesboro (August 31-September 1, 1864)
Lovejoy's Station (September 2-5, 1864)
Allatoona (October 5, 1864)
Franklin (November 30, 1864)
Nashville (December 15-16, 1864)
Mobile (March 17-April 12, 1865)

## 148.  MISSISSIPPI 4TH INFANTRY REGIMENT, STATE TROOPS

**Organization:**  Organized for six months in late 1862. Mustered out in mid-
1863.
**First Commander:**  W. C. Bromley (Colonel)
**Field Officers:**  Benjamin M. Kilgore (Major)
J. J. Stone (Lieutenant Colonel)
**Assignment:**  Hébert's Brigade, Maury's Division, 2nd Military District, De-
partment of Mississippi and East Louisiana (January-April 1863)

## 149.  MISSISSIPPI 5TH INFANTRY BATTALION

**Organization:**  Organized in 1861. Increased to a regiment and designated as
the 31st Infantry Regiment in 1862.
**First Commander:**  Jehu A. Orr (Lieutenant Colonel)
**Field Officer:**  William H. Kilpatrick (Major)

## 150.  MISSISSIPPI 5TH INFANTRY REGIMENT

*Organization:*  Organized in 1861. Field consolidation with the 3rd Infantry Battalion from July 24, 1864 to April 9, 1865. Part consolidated with the 8th and 32nd Infantry Regiments and the 3rd Infantry Battalion and designated as the 8th Infantry Battalion Consolidated at Smithfield, North Carolina on April 9, 1865. Part consolidated with the 14th and 43rd Infantry Regiment and designated as the 14th Infantry Regiment Consolidated at Smithfield, North Carolina on April 9, 1865.

*First Commander:*  Albert E. Fant (Colonel)

*Field Officers:*  John R. Dickens (Colonel)

Samuel F. M. Faucett (Major, Lieutenant Colonel)

John B. Herring (Major, Lieutenant Colonel)

James R. Moore (Major)

Adam T. Stennis (Major)

W. L. Sykes (Lieutenant Colonel)

John Weir (Major, Colonel)

*Assignments:*  Army of Pensacola, Department of Alabama and West Florida (January-March 1862)

Chalmers' Brigade, 1st Corps, 2nd Grand Division, Army of the Mississippi, Department #2 (March 1862)

Chalmers' Brigade, Withers' Division, 2nd Corps, Army of the Mississippi, Department #2 (March-June 1862)

Chalmers' Brigade, Reserve Corps, Army of the Mississippi, Department #2 (June-July 1862)

Chalmers' Brigade, Withers' Division, Army of the Mississippi, Department #2 (July-August 1862)

Chalmers' Brigade, Withers' Division, Right Wing, Army of the Mississippi, Department #2 (August 1862)

Jackson's Brigade, Withers' Division, Right Wing, Army of the Mississippi, Department #2 (November 1862)

Jackson's Brigade, Withers' Division, 1st Corps, Army of Tennessee (November-December 1862)

Jackson's Brigade, Army of Tennessee (December 1862-August 1863)

Jackson's Brigade, Cheatham's Division, 1st Corps, Army of Tennessee (August 1863-February 1864)

Jackson's Brigade, Walker's Division, 1st Corps, Army of Tennessee (February-July 1864)

Gist's Brigade, Walker's Division, 1st Corps, Army of Tennessee (July 1864)

Lowrey's Brigade, Cleburne's Division, 1st Corps, Army of Tennessee (July 1864-April 1865)

*Battles:*  Shiloh (April 6-7, 1862)

Corinth Campaign (April-June 1862)
Murfreesboro (December 31, 1862-January 3, 1863)
Tullahoma Campaign (June 1863)
Chickamauga (September 19-20, 1863)
Chattanooga Siege (September-November 1863)
Chattanooga (November 23-25, 1863)
Atlanta Campaign (May-September 1864)
Peach Tree Creek (July 20, 1864)
Atlanta (July 22, 1864)
Atlanta Siege (July-September 1864)
Franklin (November 30, 1864)
Nashville (December 15-16, 1864)
Carolinas Campaign (February-April 1865)
Bentonville (March 19-21, 1865)

## 151. MISSISSIPPI 5TH INFANTRY REGIMENT, STATE TROOPS

*Also Known As:*   5th Infantry Regiment, Minute Men

*Organization:*   Organized for six months in late 1862. Surrendered at Vicksburg, Warren County, Mississippi on July 4, 1863. Paroled at Vicksburg, Warren County, Mississippi on July 4, 1863. Apparently never reorganized.

*First Commander:*   Henry C. Robinson (Colonel)

*Field Officers:*   David W. Metts (Lieutenant Colonel)
Samuel J. Randell (Major)

*Assignments:*   1st Military District, Department of Mississippi and East Louisiana (January-April 1863)

Harris' Brigade, Mississippi State Troops [attached to Vaughn's Brigade], Smith's Division, Department of Mississippi and East Louisiana (April-July 1863)

*Battles:*   Vicksburg Campaign (May-July 1863)
Vicksburg Siege (May-July 1863)

## 152. MISSISSIPPI 6TH INFANTRY BATTALION

*Organization:*   Organized with four companies in the spring of 1862. Disbanded in the summer of 1862.

*First Commander:*   G. W. Stubbs (Lieutenant Colonel)

*Field Officer:*   John W. Jones (Major)

*Assignments:*   Department of Southern Mississippi and East Louisiana (June 1862)

2nd Sub-district, District of the Mississippi, Department #2 (June-August 1862)

3rd Sub-district, District of the Mississippi, Department #2 (September 1862)

*Battle:* Vicksburg Bombardments (May 18-July 27, 1862)

### 153. MISSISSIPPI 6TH INFANTRY BATTALION
*Organization:* This unit does not appear in the *Official Records.*
*First Commander:* G. W. Stubbs (Lieutenant Colonel)

### 154. MISSISSIPPI 6TH INFANTRY REGIMENT
*Also Known As:* 7th Infantry Regiment
*Organization:* Organized in August 1861. Reorganized on May 23, 1862. Consolidated with the 15th, 20th, and 23rd Infantry Regiments and designated as the 15th Infantry Regiment. Consolidated at Smithfield, North Carolina on April 9, 1865.
*First Commander:* John J. Thornton (Colonel)
*Field Officers:* Enoch R. Bennett (Lieutenant Colonel)
Thomas J. Borden (Major, Lieutenant Colonel)
Alfred Y. Harper (Lieutenant Colonel)
William T. Hendon (Major)
Robert Lowry (Major, Colonel)
J. R. Stevens (Major)
*Assignments:* Cleburne's Brigade, Hardee's Division, 1st Geographical Division, Department #2 (October 1861)
Cleburne's Brigade, Hardee's Division, Central Army of Kentucky, Department #2 (October 1861-March 1862)
Cleburne's Brigade, 3rd Corps, Army of the Mississippi, Department #2 (March-April 1862)
Martin's Brigade, 3rd Corps, Army of the Mississippi, Department #2 (April 1862)
Helm's Brigade, Reserve Corps, Army of the Mississippi, Department #2 (May-June 1862)
Department of Southern Mississippi and East Louisiana (June-July 1862)
Bowen's Brigade, Lovell's Division, District of the Mississippi, Department #2 (July-October 1862)
Bowen's Brigade, Lovell's Division, Department of Mississippi and East Louisiana (October-December 1862)
Scott's Brigade, Rust's Division, 1st Corps (Loring's) Army of North Mississippi, Department of Mississippi and East Louisiana (December 1862-January 1863)
Bowen's Brigade, Price's Division, Army of North Mississippi, Department of Mississippi and East Louisiana (January-February 1863)
Rust's Brigade, 3rd Military District, Department of Mississippi and East Louisiana (March-April 1863)

Tilghman's Brigade, Loring's Division, Department of Mississippi and East Louisiana (April-May 1863)

Tilghman's-Reynolds'-Adams' Brigade, Loring's Division, Department of the West (May-July 1863)

Adams' Brigade, Loring's Division, Department of Mississippi and East Louisiana (July 1863-January 1864)

Adams' Brigade, Loring's Division, Department of Alabama, Mississippi, and East Louisiana (January-May 1864)

Adams' Brigade, Loring's Division, Army of Mississippi (May-July 1864)

Adams' Brigade, Loring's Division, 3rd Corps, Army of Tennessee (July 1864-April 1865)

**Battles:**   Shiloh (April 6-7, 1862)
Corinth Campaign (April-June 1862)
Vicksburg Bombardments (May 18-July 27, 1862)
Corinth (October 3-4, 1862)
Grand Gulf (April 29, 1863)
Vicksburg Campaign (May-July 1863)
Port Gibson (May 1, 1863)
Champion Hill (May 16, 1863)
Jackson Siege (July 1863)
Atlanta Campaign (May-September 1864)
New Hope Church (May 25-June 4, 1864)
Peach Tree Creek (July 20, 1864)
Ezra Church (July 28, 1864)
Atlanta Siege (July-September 1864)
Jonesboro (August 31-September 1, 1864)
Franklin (November 30, 1864)
Nashville (December 15-16, 1864)
Carolinas Campaign (February-April 1865)

**Further Reading:**   Howell, H. Grady, *Going to Meet the Yankees: A History of the "Bloody Sixth" Mississippi Infantry C.S.A..*

## 155.   MISSISSIPPI 7TH INFANTRY BATTALION

**Also Known As:**   8th Infantry Battalion

**Organization:**   Organized in the summer of 1862.  Regiment surrendered at Vicksburg, Warren County, Mississippi on July 4, 1863.  Paroled at Vicksburg, Warren County, Mississippi in July 1863.  Declared exchanged on September 12, 1863.  Surrendered by Lieutenant Richard Taylor, commanding the Department of Alabama, Mississippi, and East Louisiana, at Citronelle, Alabama on May 4, 1865.

**First Commander:**   James S. Terral (Lieutenant Colonel)

**Field Officers:** L. B. Pardue (Lieutenant Colonel)
Joel E. Welborn (Major)

**Assignments:** Green's Brigade, Little's-Hébert's Division, Price's Corps, Army of West Tennessee, Department #2 (September-October 1862)

Green's Brigade, Hébert's Division, Price's Corps, Army of West Tennessee, Department of Mississippi and East Louisiana (October 1862)

Hébert's Brigade, Maury's Division, Price's Corps, Army of West Tennessee, Department of Mississippi and East Louisiana (October-December 1862)

Hébert's Brigade, Maury's Division, 2nd Corps, Army of North Mississippi, Department of Mississippi and East Louisiana (December 1862-January 1863)

Hébert's Brigade, Maury's Division, 2nd Military District, Department of Mississippi and East Louisiana (January-April 1863)

Hébert's Brigade, Maury's-Forney's Division, Department of Mississippi and East Louisiana (April-July 1863)

Mackall's Brigade, Department of the Gulf (February 1864)

Sears' Brigade, Department of Alabama, Mississippi, and East Louisiana (March-May 1864)

Sears' Brigade, Army of Mississippi (May 1864)

Sear's Brigade, French's Division, Army of Mississippi (May-July 1864)

Sears' Brigade, French's Division, 3rd Corps, Army of Tennessee (July 1864-January 1865)

Sears' Brigade, French's Division, District of the Gulf, Department of Alabama, Mississippi, and East Louisiana (January-April 1865)

Sears' Brigade, French's Division, Department of Alabama, Mississippi, and East Louisiana (April-May 1865)

**Battles:** Iuka (September 19, 1862)
Corinth (October 3-4, 1862)
Vicksburg Campaign (May-July 1863)
Vicksburg Siege (May-July 1863)
Atlanta Campaign (May-September 1864)
Cassville (May 19-22, 1864)
New Hope Church (May 25-June 4, 1864)
Lattimer's Mills (June 20, 1864)
Kennesaw Mountain (June 27, 1864)
Atlanta Siege (July-September 1864)
Smyrna Campground (July 4, 1864)
Chattahoochee River (July 5-17, 1864)
Atlanta (July 22, 1864)
Peach Tree Creek (July 20, 1864)
Ezra Church (July 28, 1864)

Jonesboro (August 31-September 1, 1864)
Lovejoy's Station (September 2-5, 1864)
Allatoona (October 5, 1864)
Franklin (November 30, 1864)
Nashville (December 15-16, 1864)
Mobile (March 17-April 12, 1865)

## 156.  MISSISSIPPI 7TH INFANTRY REGIMENT

**Organization:**  Organized in 1861. Field consolidation with the 9th Infantry Regiment at various times from November 1863 to April 9, 1865. Consolidated with the 9th, 10th, 41st, and 44th Infantry Regiments and the 9th Sharpshooters Battalion and designated as the 9th Infantry Regiment Consolidated at Smithfield, North Carolina on April 9, 1865.

**First Commander:**  Enos J. Goode (Colonel)
**Field Officers:**  William H. Bishop (Colonel)
R. S. Carter (Major, Lieutenant Colonel)
Benjamin F. Johns (Major, Lieutenant Colonel)
James H. Mayson (Lieutenant Colonel, Colonel)
Andrew G. Mills (Lieutenant Colonel)
Henry Pope (Major)

**Assignments:**  Department #1 (December 1861-February 1862)
1st Geographical Division, Department #2 (February-March 1862)
Chalmers' Brigade, 1st Corps, 2nd Grand Division, Army of the Mississippi, Department #2 (March 1862)
Chalmers' Brigade, Withers' Division, 2nd Corps, Army of the Mississippi, Department #2 (March-June 1862)
Chalmers' Brigade, Reserve Corps, Army of the Mississippi, Department #2 (June-July 1862)
Chalmers' Brigade, Withers' Division, Army of the Mississippi, Department #2 (July-August 1862)
Chalmers' Brigade, Withers' Division, Right Wing, Army of the Mississippi, Department #2 (August-October 1862)
Jackson's Brigade, Withers' Division, Right Wing, Army of Northern Virginia (November 1862)
Jackson's Brigade, Withers' Division, 1st Corps, Army of Tennessee (November 1862)
Chalmers'-White's-Anderson's Brigade, Withers'-Hindman's Division, 1st Corps, Army of Tennessee (November 1862-December 1863)
Anderson's-Tucker's-Sharp's Brigade, Hindman's-Anderson's-Johnson's-D. H. Hill's Division, 2nd Corps, Army of Tennessee (December 1863-April 1865)

**Battles:**  Shiloh (April 6-7, 1862)

Corinth Campaign (April-June 1862)
Munfordville (September 17, 1862)
Murfreesboro (December 31, 1862-January 3, 1863)
Rover (February 13, 1863)
Tullahoma Campaign (June 1863)
Chickamauga (September 19-20, 1863)
Chattanooga Siege (September-November 1863)
Chattanooga (November 23-25, 1863)
Atlanta Campaign (May-September 1864)
Resaca (May 14-15, 1864)
New Hope Church (May 25-June 4, 1864)
Atlanta Siege (July-September 1864)
Franklin (November 30, 1864)
Nashville (December 15-16, 1864)
Carolinas Campaign (February-April 1865)

## 157. MISSISSIPPI 8TH INFANTRY BATTALION
*See:* MISSISSIPPI 7TH INFANTRY BATTALION

## 158. MISSISSIPPI 8TH INFANTRY BATTALION, CONSOLIDATED
**Organization:** Organized by the consolidation of the 3rd Infantry Battalion, the 8th and 32nd Infantry Regiments, and part of the 5th Infantry Regiment at Smithfield, North Carolina on April 9, 1865.
**Assignment:** Sharp's Brigade, D. H. Hill's Division, 2nd Corps, Army of Tennessee (April 1865)
**Battle:** Carolinas Campaign (February-April 1865)

## 159. MISSISSIPPI 8TH INFANTRY BATTALION, SHARPSHOOTERS
*See:* MISSISSIPPI 9TH INFANTRY BATTALION, SHARPSHOOTERS

## 160. MISSISSIPPI 8TH INFANTRY REGIMENT
**Organization:** Organized in 1861. Field consolidation with the 32nd Infantry Regiment from July 24, 1864 to April 9, 1865. Consolidated with the 3rd Infantry Battalion, 32nd Infantry Regiment and part of the 5th Infantry Regiment and designated as the 8th Infantry Battalion. Consolidated at Smithfield, North Carolina on April 9, 1865.
**First Commander:** Guilford G. Flynt (Colonel)
**Field Officers:** Greene C. Chandler (Colonel)
James T. Gates (Lieutenant Colonel)
Aden McNeill (Lieutenant Colonel)
Andrew E. Moody (Major)

George F. Peek (Major)

John F. Smith (Major, Lieutenant Colonel)

William Watkins (Major)

John C. Wilkinson (Colonel)

**Assignments:** Army of Pensacola, Department of Alabama and West Florida (January-March 1862)

Department of Alabama and West Florida (March-April 1862)

Jackson's Brigade, Withers' Division, Right Wing, Army of the Mississippi, Department #2 (August-November 1862)

Jackson's Brigade, Withers' Division, 1st Corps, Army of Tennessee (November-December 1862)

Jackson's Brigade, Army of Tennessee (December 1862-August 1863)

Jackson's Brigade, Cheatham's Division, 1st Corps, Army of Tennessee (August 1863-February 1864)

Jackson's Brigade, Walker's Division, 1st Corps, Army of Tennessee (February-July 1864)

Gist's Brigade, Walker's Division, 1st Corps, Army of Tennessee (July 1864)

Lowrey's Brigade, Cleburne's Division, 1st Corps, Army of Tennessee (July 1864-April 1865)

**Battles:** Murfreesboro (December 31, 1862-January 3, 1863)

Tullahoma Campaign (June 1863)

Chickamauga (September 19-20, 1863)

Chattanooga Siege (September-November 1863)

Chattanooga (November 23-25, 1863)

Atlanta Campaign (May-September 1864)

Peach Tree Creek (July 20, 1864)

Atlanta (July 22, 1864)

Atlanta Siege (July-September 1864)

Franklin (November 30, 1864)

Nashville (December 15-16, 1864)

Carolinas Campaign (February-April 1865)

Bentonville (March 19-21, 1865)

## 161. MISSISSIPPI 9TH INFANTRY BATTALION, SHARPSHOOTERS

**Organization:** Organized in the summer of 1862. Field consolidation with the 10th and 44th Infantry Regiments from September 1864 to April 9, 1865. Consolidated with the 7th, 9th, 10th, 41st, and 44th Infantry Regiments and designated as the 9th Infantry Regiment Consolidated at Smithfield, North Carolina on April 9, 1865.

**First Commander:** William C. Richards (Major)

*Assignments:* Chalmers' Brigade, Withers' Division, Right Wing, Army of
the Mississippi, Department #2 (September-November 1862)
Chalmers'-Anderson's Brigade, Withers'-Hindman's Division, 1st Corps, Army
of Tennessee (November 1862-November 1863)
Anderson's-Tucker's-Sharp's Brigade, Hindman's-Anderson's-Johnson's-D.H.
Hill's Division, 2nd Corps, Army of Tennessee (November 1863-April 1865)
*Battles:* Munfordville (September 17, 1862)
Murfreesboro (December 31, 1862-January 3, 1863)
Rover (February 13, 1863)
Tullahoma Campaign (June 1863)
Chickamauga (September 19-20, 1863)
Chattanooga Siege (September-November 1863)
Chattanooga (November 23-25, 1863)
Atlanta Campaign (May-September 1864)
Resaca (May 14-15, 1864)
New Hope Church (May 25-June 4, 1864)
Atlanta Siege (July-September 1864)
Franklin (November 30, 1864)
Nashville (December 15-16, 1864)
Carolinas Campaign (February-April 1865)

## 162. MISSISSIPPI 9TH INFANTRY REGIMENT

*Organization:* Organized in April 1861. Field consolidation with the 7th
Infantry Regiment at various times from November 1863 to April 9, 1865.
Consolidated with the 7th, 10th, 41st, and 44th Infantry Regiments and the
9th Sharpshooters Battalion and designated as the 9th Infantry Regiment
Consolidated at Smithfield, North Carolina on April 9, 1865.
*First Commander:* James R. Chalmers (Colonel)
*Field Officers:* James L. Autry (Lieutenant Colonel, Colonel)
Albert R. Bowdre (Major)
Solomon S. Calhoon (Lieutenant Colonel)
J. M. Hicks (Major)
Thomas H. Lynam (Major, Lieutenant Colonel)
Andrew G. Mills (Major)
William A. Rankin (Lieutenant Colonel)
William C. Richards (Colonel)
Jesse E. White (Major)
Thomas W. White (Colonel)
Francis E. Whitfield (Major, Lieutenant Colonel)
*Assignments:* Department of West Florida (September-October 1861)
Department of Alabama and West Florida (October 1861)

Army of Pensacola, Department of Alabama and West Florida (October 1861-February 1862)

Chalmers' Brigade, 1st Corps, 2nd Grand Division, Army of the Mississippi, Department #2 (March 1862)

Chalmers' Brigade, Withers' Division, 2nd Corps, Army of the Mississippi, Department #2 (March-June 1862)

Chalmers' Brigade, Reserve Corps, Army of the Mississippi, Department #2 (June-July 1862)

Chalmers' Brigade, Withers' Division, Army of the Mississippi, Department #2 (July-August 1862)

Chalmers' Brigade, Withers' Division, Right Wing, Army of the Mississippi, Department #2 (August-October 1862)

Jackson's Brigade, Withers' Division, Right Wing, Army of Northern Virginia (November 1862)

Jackson's Brigade, Withers' Division, 1st Corps, Army of Tennessee (November 1862)

Chalmers'-White's-Anderson's Brigade, Withers'-Hindman's Division, 1st Corps, Army of Tennessee (November 1862-December 1863)

Anderson's-Tucker's-Sharp's Brigade, Hindman's-Anderson's-Johnson's-D. H. Hill's Division, 2nd Corps, Army of Tennessee (December 1863-April 1865)

**Battles:** Santa Rosa Island (October 9, 1861)

Shiloh (April 6-7, 1862)

Corinth Campaign (April-June 1862)

Kentucky Campaign (August-October 1862)

Munfordville (September 17, 1862)

Murfreesboro (December 31, 1862-January 3, 1863)

Rover (February 13, 1863)

Tullahoma Campaign (June 1863)

Chickamauga (September 19-20, 1863)

Chattanooga Siege (September-November 1863)

Chattanooga (November 23-25, 1863)

Atlanta Campaign (May-September 1864)

Resaca (May 14-15, 1864)

New Hope Church (May 25-June 4, 1864)

Atlanta Siege (July-September 1864)

Franklin (November 30, 1864)

Nashville (December 15-16, 1864)

Carolinas Campaign (February-April 1865)

## 163.   MISSISSIPPI 9TH INFANTRY REGIMENT, CONSOLIDATED

*Organization:*  Organized by the consolidation of the 7th, 9th, 10th, 41st, and 44th Infantry Regiments and the 9th Sharpshooters Battalion at Smithfield, North Carolina on April 9, 1865.  Surrendered by General Joseph E. Johnston at Durham Station, Orange County, North Carolina on April 26, 1865.

*First Commander:*  William C. Richards (Colonel)

*Field Officers:*  Solomon S. Calhoon (Lieutenant Colonel)

Thomas H. Lyman (Major)

*Assignment:*  Sharp's Brigade, D. H. Hill's Division, 2nd Corps, Army of Tennessee (April 1865)

*Battle:*  Carolinas Campaign (February-April 1865)

## 164.   MISSISSIPPI 10TH INFANTRY BATTALION, SHARPSHOOTERS

*See:* MISSISSIPPI 1ST INFANTRY BATTALION, SHARPSHOOTERS

## 165.   MISSISSIPPI 10TH INFANTRY REGIMENT

*Organization:*  Organized in April 1861.  Field consolidation with the 44th Infantry Regiment at various times from November 1863 to April 9, 1865. Additional field consolidation with the 9th Sharpshooters Battalion from September 1864 to April 9, 1865.  Consolidated with the 7th, 9th, 41st, and 44th Infantry Regiments and the 9th Sharpshooters Battalion and designated as the 9th Infantry Regiment Consolidated at Smithfield, North Carolina on April 9, 1865.

*First Commander:*  Seaborne M. Phillips (Colonel)

*Field Officers:*  James Barr, Jr. (Major, Lieutenant Colonel, Colonel)

James G. Bullard (Lieutenant Colonel)

Joseph R. Davis (Lieutenant Colonel)

James M. Dotson (Major)

Edward H. Gregory (Major)

George B. Myers (Lieutenant Colonel)

Robert A. Smith (Colonel)

James M. Walker (Lieutenant Colonel, Colonel)

*Assignments:*  Department of West Florida (September-October 1861)

Department of Alabama and West Florida (October 1861)

Army of Pensacola, Department of Alabama and West Florida (October 1861-February 1862)

Chalmers' Brigade, 1st Corps, 2nd Grand Division, Army of the Mississippi, Department #2 (March 1862)

Chalmers' Brigade, Withers' Division, 2nd Corps, Army of the Mississippi, Department #2 (March-June 1862)

Chalmers' Brigade, Reserve Corps, Army of the Mississippi, Department #2 (June-July 1862)

Chalmers' Brigade, Withers' Division, Army of the Mississippi, Department #2 (July-August 1862)

Chalmers' Brigade, Withers' Division, Right Wing, Army of the Mississippi, Department #2 (August-October 1862)

Jackson's Brigade, Withers' Division, Right Wing, Army of Northern Virginia (November 1862)

Jackson's Brigade, Withers' Division, 1st Corps, Army of Tennessee (November 1862)

Chalmers'-White's-Anderson's Brigade, Withers'-Hindman's Division, 1st Corps, Army of Tennessee (November 1862-December 1863)

Anderson's-Tucker's-Sharp's Brigade, Hindman's-Anderson's-Johnson's-D. H. Hill's Division, 2nd Corps, Army of Tennessee (December 1863-April 1865)

**Battles:**  Santa Rosa Island (October 9, 1861)

Shiloh (April 6-7, 1862)

Corinth Campaign (April-June 1862)

Kentucky Campaign (August-October 1862)

Munfordville (September 17, 1862)

Murfreesboro (December 31, 1862-January 3, 1863)

Rover (February 13, 1863)

Tullahoma Campaign (June 1863)

Chickamauga (September 19-20, 1863)

Chattanooga Siege (September-November 1863)

Chattanooga (November 23-25, 1863)

Atlanta Campaign (May-September 1864)

Resaca (May 14-15, 1864)

New Hope Church (May 25-June 4, 1864)

Atlanta Siege (July-September 1864)

Franklin (November 30, 1864)

Nashville (December 15-16, 1864)

Carolinas Campaign (February-April 1865)

## 166.  MISSISSIPPI 11TH INFANTRY REGIMENT

**Organization:**  Organized on May 4, 1861.  Reorganized on April 21, 1862. Surrendered at Appomattox Court House, Virginia on April 9, 1865.

**First Commander:**  William H. Moore (Colonel)

**Field Officers:**  Samuel F. Butler (Major, Lieutenant Colonel)

Taliaferro S. Evans (Major)

Alexander H. Franklin (Lieutenant Colonel)

Francis M. Green (Major, Colonel)

William B. Lowry (Major, Lieutenant Colonel)
Reuben O. Reynolds (Major, Colonel)
George W. Shannon (Lieutenant Colonel)
**Assignments:**  Harpers Ferry (May-June 1861)
Bee's Brigade, Army of the Shenandoah (June-July 1861)
Bee's-Whiting's Brigade, 2nd Corps, Army of the Potomac (July-October 1861)
Whiting's Brigade, Forces near Dumfries [Whiting's Command], 2nd Corps, Potomac District, Department of Northern Virginia (October 1861-January 1862)
Whiting's Brigade, Forces near Dumfries [Whiting's Command], Potomac District, Department of Northern Virginia (January-March 1862)
Whiting's Brigade, Whiting's Division, Army of Northern Virginia (March-June 1862)
Whiting's Brigade, Whiting's Division, Valley District, Department of Northern Virginia (June 1862)
Whiting's Brigade, Whiting's Division, 2nd Corps, Army of Northern Virginia (June-July 1862)
Whiting's-Law's Brigade, Whiting's-Hood's Division, 1st Corps, Army of Northern Virginia (July-September 1862)
Davis' Brigade, Unattached, Department of North Carolina and Southern Virginia (December 1862)
Davis' Brigade, French's Command, Department of North Carolina and Southern Virginia (December 1862-February 1863)
Davis' Brigade, Department of Southern Virginia (May 1863)
Davis' Brigade, Department of North Carolina (May 1863)
Davis' Brigade, Heth's Division, 3rd Corps, Army of Northern Virginia (May 1863-April 1865)
**Battles:**  1st Bull Run [two companies] (July 21, 1861)
Yorktown Siege (April-May 1862)
Seven Pines (May 31-June 1, 1862)
Seven Days Battles (June 25-July 1, 1862)
Gaines' Mill (June 27, 1862)
Malvern Hill (July 1, 1862)
2nd Bull Run (August 28-30, 1862)
South Mountain (September 14, 1862)
Antietam (September 17, 1862)
Gettysburg (July 1-3, 1863)
Falling Waters (July 14, 1863)
Bristoe Campaign (October 1863)
Mine Run Campaign (November-December 1863)
The Wilderness (May 5-6, 1864)

Spotsylvania Court House (May 8-21, 1864)

North Anna (May 23-26, 1864)

Cold Harbor (June 1-3, 1864)

Petersburg Siege (June 1864-April 1865)

Hatcher's Run (February 5-7, 1865)

Appomattox Court House (April 9, 1865)

**Further Reading:** Brown, Maud Morrow, *The University Greys, Company A, 11th Mississippi Regiment, Army of Northern Virginia.*

### 167. MISSISSIPPI 12TH INFANTRY REGIMENT

**Organization:** Organized in May 1861. Surrendered at Appomattox Court House, Virginia on April 9, 1865.

**First Commander:** Richard Griffith (Colonel)

**Field Officers:** James R. Bell (Major)

John R. Dickens (Major)

Merrie B. Harris (Lieutenant Colonel, Colonel)

Henry Hughes (Colonel)

William H. Lilly (Major)

William H. Taylor (Lieutenant Colonel, Colonel)

Samuel B. Thomas (Major, Lieutenant Colonel)

**Assignments:** Ewell's Brigade, 1st Corps, Army of the Potomac (July-October 1861)

Ewell's Brigade, Van Dorn's Division, 1st Corps, Army of the Potomac (October 1861)

Ewell's-Rodes' Brigade, Van Dorn's Division, 1st Corps, Potomac District, Department of Northern Virginia (October 1861-January 1862)

Rodes' Brigade, Van Dorn's-Early's Division, Potomac District, Department of Northern Virginia (January-March 1862)

Rodes' Brigade, D. H. Hill's Division, Department of Northern Virginia (March-April 1862)

Rodes' Brigade, Early's Division, D. H. Hill's Command, Department of Northern Virginia (April-May 1862)

Rodes' Brigade, D. H. Hill's Division, Army of Northern Virginia (May-June 1862)

Featherston's Brigade, Longstreet's Division, Army of Northern Virginia (June 1862)

Featherston's Brigade, Longstreet's Division, 1st Corps, Army of Northern Virginia (June-August 1862)

Featherston's Brigade, Wilcox's Division, 1st Corps, Army of Northern Virginia (August-September 1862)

Featherston's-Posey's Brigade, R. H. Anderson's Division, 1st Corps, Army of
   Northern Virginia (September 1862-May 1863)
Posey's-Harris' Brigade, R. H. Anderson's-Mahone's Division, 3rd Corps, Army
   of Northern Virginia (May 1863-April 1865)
**Battles:**  Yorktown Siege (April-May 1862)
Williamsburg (May 5, 1862)
Seven Pines (May 31-June 1, 1862)
Seven Days Battles (June 25-July 1, 1862)
Gaines' Mill (June 27, 1862)
Frayser's Farm (June 30, 1862)
Kelly's Ford [skirmish] (August 21, 1862)
2nd Bull Run (August 28-30, 1862)
Antietam (September 17, 1862)
Fredericksburg (December 13, 1862)
Chancellorsville (May 1-4, 1863)
Gettysburg (July 1-3, 1863)
Bristoe Campaign (October 1863)
Mine Run Campaign (November-December 1863)
The Wilderness (May 5-6, 1864)
Spotsylvania Court House (May 8-21, 1864)
North Anna (May 23-26, 1864)
Cold Harbor (June 1-3, 1864)
Petersburg Siege (June 1864-April 1865)
Appomattox Court House (April 9, 1865)

## 168.  MISSISSIPPI 13TH INFANTRY BATTALION
*See:* MISSISSIPPI, 1ST INFANTRY BATTALION, STATE TROOPS

## 169.  MISSISSIPPI 13TH INFANTRY REGIMENT
**Organization:**  Organized in May 1861.  Reorganized on April 26, 1862.
Surrendered at Appomattox Court House, Virginia on April 9, 1865.
**First Commander:**  William Barksdale (Colonel)
**Field Officers:**  John M. Bradley (Major, Lieutenant Colonel)
James W. Carter (Lieutenant Colonel, Colonel)
George L. Donald (Major)
Isham Harrison, Jr. (Major)
Kennon McElroy (Major, Lieutenant Colonel, Colonel)
Alfred G. O'Brien (Major, Lieutenant Colonel)
Mackerness H. Whitaker (Lieutenant Colonel)
**Assignments:**  Early's Brigade, Army of the Potomac (July 1861)
Early's Brigade, 1st Corps, Army of the Potomac (July 1861)

Evans' Brigade, 1st Corps, Army of the Potomac (July-October 1861)

Evans'-Griffith's Brigade, 1st Corps, Potomac District, Department of Northern Virginia (October-November 1861)

Griffith's Brigade, Forces at Leesburg [D. H. Hill's Division], Potomac District, Department of Northern Virginia (January-March 1862)

Griffith's Brigade, McLaws' Division, Magruder's Command, Department of Northern Virginia (April-May 1862)

Griffith's Brigade, Magruder's Division, Army of Northern Virginia (May-June 1862)

Griffith's-Barksdale's Brigade, Magruder's Division, Magruder's Command, Army of Northern Virginia (June-July 1862)

Barksdale's-Humphreys' Brigade, McLaws' Division, 1st Corps, (July 1862-September 1863)

Humphreys' Brigade, McLaws' Division, Longstreet's Corps, Army of Tennessee (September-November 1863)

Humphreys' Brigade, McLaws'-Kershaw's Division, Department of East Tennessee (November 1863-April 1864)

Humphreys' Brigade, Kershaw's Division, 1st Corps, Army of Northern Virginia (April-August 1864)

Humphreys' Brigade, Kershaw's Division, Valley District, Department of Northern Virginia (August-October 1864)

Humphreys' Brigade, Kershaw's Division, 1st Corps, Army of Northern Virginia (November 1864-April 1865)

**Battles:**   1st Bull Run (July 21, 1861)

Ball's Bluff [Company D] (October 21, 1861)

Edwards' Ferry [Companies G & K] (October 22, 1861)

Yorktown Siege (April-May 1862)

Seven Days Battles (June 25-July 1, 1862)

Malvern Hill (July 1, 1862)

Harpers Ferry (September 12-15, 1862)

Maryland Heights (September 13, 1862)

Antietam (September 17, 1862)

Fredericksburg (December 13, 1862)

Chancellorsville (May 1-4, 1863)

Gettysburg (July 1-3, 1863)

Chickamauga (September 19-20, 1863)

Chattanooga Siege (September-November 1863)

Knoxville Siege (November-December 1863)

The Wilderness (May 5-6, 1864)

Spotsylvania Court House (May 8-21, 1864)

North Anna (May 23-26, 1864)

Cold Harbor (June 1-3, 1864)
Petersburg Siege (June 1864-April 1865)
Cedar Creek (October 19, 1864)
Petersburg Siege (June 1864-April 1865)
Sayler's Creek (April 6, 1865)
Appomattox Court House (April 9, 1865)
**Further Reading:** McNeily, J. S., *Barksdale's Mississippi Brigade at Gettysburg.*
Dinkins, James, *1861-1865 by an "Old Johnny".*

## 170. MISSISSIPPI 14TH INFANTRY REGIMENT

*Organization:* Organized in the spring of 1861. Surrendered at Fort Donelson on February 16, 1862. Exchanged ca. August 27, 1862. Consolidated with the 43rd Infantry Regiment and part of the 5th Infantry Regiment and designated as the 14th Infantry Regiment Consolidated at Smithfield, North Carolina on April 9, 1865.
*First Commander:* William E. Baldwin (Colonel)
*Field Officers:* George W. Abert (Lieutenant Colonel, Colonel)
Washington L. Doss (Major, Lieutenant Colonel, Colonel)
P. B. Dugan (Major)
Robert J. Lawrence (Major, Lieutenant Colonel)
Marion E. Norris (Lieutenant Colonel)
*Assignments:* District of East Tennessee, Department #2 (September-October 1861)
Baldwin's Brigade, Buckner's Division, Central Army of Kentucky, Department #2 (October 1861-February 1862)
Baldwin's Brigade, Buckner's Division, Fort Donelson, Department #2 (February 1862)
Baldwin's Brigade, Tilghman's Division, 1st Corps, Army of West Tennessee, Department of Mississippi and East Louisiana (December 1862)
Baldwin's Brigade, Tilghman's Division, 1st Corps, Army of North Mississippi, Department of Mississippi and East Louisiana (December 1862-January 1863)
Tilghman's Brigade, Loring's Division, Army of North Mississippi, Department of Mississippi and East Louisiana (January 1863)
Tilghman's Brigade, Loring's Division, 2nd Military District, Department of Mississippi and East Louisiana (January-February 1863)
4th Military District, Department of Mississippi and East Louisiana (April-May 1863)
Gist's Brigade, Department of the West (May 1863)
Gist's Brigade, Walker's Division, Department of the West (June 1863)
Adams' Brigade, Loring's Division, Department of the West (July 1863)

Adams' Brigade, Loring's Division, Department of Mississippi and East Louisiana (July 1863-January 1864)

Adams' Brigade, Loring's Division, Department of Alabama, Mississippi, and East Louisiana (January-May 1864)

Adams' Brigade, Loring's Division, Army of Mississippi (May-July 1864)

Adams' Brigade, Loring's Division, 3rd Corps, Army of Tennessee (July 1864-April 1865)

**Battles:** Fort Donelson (February 12-16, 1862)

Coffeeville (December 5, 1862)

Vicksburg Campaign (May-July 1863)

Jackson (May 14, 1863)

Jackson Siege (July 1863)

Meridian Campaign (February-March 1864)

Atlanta Campaign (May-September 1864)

New Hope Church (May 25-June 4, 1864)

Peach Tree Creek (July 20, 1864)

Ezra Church (July 28, 1864)

Atlanta Siege (July-September 1864)

Jonesboro (August 31-September 1, 1864)

Franklin (November 30, 1864)

Nashville (December 15-16, 1864)

Carolinas Campaign (February-April 1865)

## 171. MISSISSIPPI 14TH INFANTRY REGIMENT, CONSOLIDATED

**Organization:** Organized by the consolidation of the 14th and 43rd Infantry Regiments and part of the 5th Infantry Regiment at Smithfield, North Carolina on April 9, 1865.

**First Commander:** Robert J. Lawrence (Colonel)

**Assignment:** Lowry's Brigade, Loring's Division, 3rd Corps, Army of Tennessee (April 1865)

**Battle:** Carolinas Campaign (February-April 1865)

## 172. MISSISSIPPI 15TH INFANTRY BATTALION, SHARPSHOOTERS

**Organization:** Organized with two companies in the fall of 1862. Apparently broken up in early 1864.

**First Commander:** A. T. Hawkins (Major)

**Assignments:** Wood's-Lowrey's Brigade, Cleburne's Division, 2nd Corps, Army of Tennessee (December 1862-November 1863)

Lowrey's Brigade, Cleburne's Division, 1st Corps, Army of Tennessee (November 1863-February 1864)

**Battles:** Murfreesboro (December 31, 1862-January 3, 1863)
Tullahoma Campaign (June 1863)
Chickamauga (September 19-20, 1863)
Chattanooga Siege (September-November 1863)
Chattanooga (November 23-25, 1863)
Dalton (February 22-27, 1864)

## 173. MISSISSIPPI 15TH INFANTRY REGIMENT

**Organization:** Organized in the spring of 1861. Consolidated with the 6th, 20th, and 23rd Infantry Regiments and designated as the 15th Infantry Regiment Consolidated at Smithfield, North Carolina on April 9, 1865.

**First Commander:** Winfield S. Statham (Colonel)

**Field Officers:** James R. Binford (Major, Lieutenant Colonel)
William F. Brantley (Major)
Michael Farrell (Lieutenant Colonel, Colonel)
J. W. Hemphill (Lieutenant Colonel)
Russell G. Prewitt (Major)
Lamkin S. Terry (Major)
Edward C. Walthall (Lieutenant Colonel)

**Assignments:** District of East Tennessee, Department #2 (September 1861-January 1862)

Zollicoffer's Brigade, District of East Tennessee, Department #2 (January-February 1862)

Statham's Brigade, Crittenden's Division, Central Army of Kentucky, Department #2 (February-March 1862)

Statham's Brigade, Reserve Corps, Army of the Mississippi, Department #2 (March-June 1862)

Statham's Brigade, Breckinridge's Division, Department of Southern Mississippi and East Louisiana (June-July 1862)

Statham's-Smith's Brigade, Breckinridge's Division, District of the Mississippi, Department #2 (July 1862)

Smith's Brigade, Clark's Division, Breckinridge's Command, District of the Mississippi, Department #2 (July-August 1862)

Bowen's Brigade, Lovell's Division, District of the Mississippi, Department #2 (September-October 1862)

Bowen's Brigade, Lovell's Division, Department of Mississippi and East Louisiana (October-December 1862)

Scott's Brigade, Rust's Division, 1st Corps (Loring's), Army of North Mississippi, Department of Mississippi and East Louisiana (December 1862-January 1863)

Bowen's Brigade, Price's Division, Army of North Mississippi, Department of Mississippi and East Louisiana (January-February 1863)

Rust's Brigade, 3rd Military District, Department of Mississippi and East Louisiana (March-April 1863)

Tilghman's Brigade, Loring's Division, Department of Mississippi and East Louisiana (April-May 1863)

Tilghman's-Reynolds'-Adams' Brigade, Loring's Division, Department of the West (May-July 1863)

Adams' Brigade, Loring's Division, Department of Mississippi and East Louisiana (July 1863-January 1864)

Adams' Brigade, Loring's Division, Department of Alabama, Mississippi, and East Louisiana (January-May 1864)

Adams' Brigade, Loring's Division, Army of Mississippi (May-July 1864)

Adams' Brigade, Loring's Division, 3rd Corps, Army of Tennessee (July 1864-April 1865)

**Battles:**  Laurel Bridge (September 26, 1861)

Mill Springs (January 19, 1862)

Shiloh (April 6-7, 1862)

Corinth Campaign (April-June 1862)

Baton Rouge [in reserve] (August 5, 1862)

Corinth (October 3-4, 1862)

Vicksburg Bombardments (May 18-July 27, 1862)

Vicksburg Campaign (May-July 1863)

Champion Hill (May 16, 1863)

Jackson Siege (July 1863)

Meridian Campaign (February-March 1864)

Atlanta Campaign (May-September 1864)

New Hope Church (May 25-June 4, 1864)

Peach Tree Creek (July 20, 1864)

Ezra Church (July 28, 1864)

Atlanta Siege (July-September 1864)

Jonesboro (August 31-September 1, 1864)

Franklin (November 30, 1864)

Nashville (December 15-16, 1864)

Carolinas Campaign (February-April 1865)

Bentonville (March 19-21, 1865)

## 174.  MISSISSIPPI 15TH INFANTRY REGIMENT, CONSOLIDATED

*Organization:*  Organized by the consolidation of the 6th, 15th, 20th, and 23rd Infantry Regiments at Smithfield, North Carolina on April 9, 1865. Surrendered by General Joseph E. Johnston at Durham Station, Orange County, North Carolina on April 26, 1865.

**First Commander:**   Thomas B. Graham (Lieutenant Colonel)

**Assignment:**   Lowry's Brigade, Loring's Division, 3rd Corps, Army of Tennessee (April 1865)

**Battle:**   Carolinas Campaign (February-April 1865)

## 175.   MISSISSIPPI 16TH INFANTRY REGIMENT

**Organization:**   Organized at Corinth on June 8, 1861. Reorganized on April 28, 1862. Surrendered at Appomattox Court House, Virginia on April 9, 1865.

**First Commander:**   Carnot Posey (Colonel)

**Field Officers:**   Senaca M. Bain (Lieutenant Colonel)

Samuel E. Baker (Major, Colonel)

Thomas J. Bankston (Major)

Robert Clarke (Lieutenant Colonel)

Edward C. Councell (Major, Colonel)

Abram M. Feltus (Lieutenant Colonel)

James J. Shannon (Lieutenant Colonel)

Thomas R. Stockdale (Major)

**Assignments:**   Crittenden's Brigade, 1st Corps, Army of the Potomac (September-October 1861)

Crittenden's Brigade, 1st Corps, Potomac District, Department of Northern Virginia (October-November 1861)

Crittenden's-Trimble's Brigade, E. K. Smith's Division, 1st Corps, Potomac District, Department of Northern Virginia (November 1861-January 1862)

Trimble's Brigade, E. K. Smith's-Ewell's Division, Potomac District, Department of Northern Virginia (January-March 1862)

Trimble's Brigade, Ewell's Division, Department of Northern Virginia (March-May 1862)

Trimble's Brigade, Ewell's Division, Valley District, Department of Northern Virginia (May-June 1862)

Trimble's Brigade, Ewell's Division, 2nd Corps, Army of Northern Virginia (June-July 1862)

Featherston's Brigade, Longstreet's Division, 1st Corps, Army of Northern Virginia (June-August 1862)

Featherston's Brigade, Wilcox's Division, 1st Corps, Army of Northern Virginia (August-September 1862)

Featherston's-Posey's Brigade, R. H. Anderson's Division, 1st Corps, Army of Northern Virginia (September 1862-May 1863)

Posey's-Harris' Brigade, R. H. Anderson's-Mahone's Division, 3rd Corps, Army of Northern Virginia (May 1863-April 1865)

**Battles:**  Shenandoah Valley Campaign (May 1862)
Cross Keys (June 8, 1862)
Seven Days Battles (June 25-July 1, 1862)
Gaines' Mill (June 27, 1862)
Malvern Hill (July 1, 1862)
Kelly's Ford [skirmish] (August 21, 1862)
2nd Bull Run (August 28-30, 1862)
Antietam (September 17, 1862)
Fredericksburg (December 13, 1862)
Chancellorsville (May 1-4, 1863)
Gettysburg (July 1-3, 1863)
Bristoe Campaign (October 1863)
Mine Run Campaign (November-December 1863)
The Wilderness (May 5-6, 1864)
Spotsylvania Court House (May 8-21, 1864)
North Anna (May 23-26, 1864)
Cold Harbor (June 1-3, 1864)
Petersburg Siege (June 1864-April 1865)
Appomattox Court House (April 9, 1865)
**Further Reading:**  Lightsey, Ada Christine, *The Veteran's Story* . . . .

## 176.  MISSISSIPPI 17TH INFANTRY REGIMENT

**Organization:**  Organized in June 1861. Mustered into Confederate service in
June 1861. Reorganized on April 26, 1862. Surrendered at Appomattox Court
House, Virginia on April 9, 1865.
**First Commander:**  Winfield S. Featherston (Colonel)
**Field Officers:**  Gwen R. Cherry (Major, Lieutenant Colonel)
William L. Duff (Major)
John C. Fizer (Lieutenant Colonel, Colonel)
William D. Holder (Colonel)
Robert L. Knox (Major)
John M. Lyles (Major)
John McGuirk (Lieutenant Colonel)
Andrew J. Pulliam (Lieutenant Colonel, Colonel)
Edward W. Upshaw (Major)
**Assignments:**  D. R. Jones' Brigade, Army of the Potomac (June-July 1861)
D. R. Jones' Brigade, 1st Corps, Army of the Potomac (July 1861)
Evans' Brigade, 1st Corps, Army of the Potomac (July-October 1861)
Evans'-Griffith's Brigade, Forces at Leesburg [D. H. Hill's Division], Potomac
    District, Department of Northern Virginia (October 1861-March 1862)

H. Cobb's Brigade, McLaws'-Magruder's Division, Department of Northern
Virginia (April-May 1862)

Griffith's-Barksdale's Brigade, Magruder's Division, Army of Northern Virginia
(June-July 1862)

Barksdale's-Humphreys' Brigade, McLaws' Division, 1st Corps, Army of Northern Virginia (July 1862-September 1863)

Humphreys' Brigade, McLaws' Division, Longstreet's Corps, Army of Tennessee (September-November 1863)

Humphreys' Brigade, McLaws'-Kershaw's Division, Department of East Tennessee (November 1863-April 1864)

Humphreys' Brigade, Kershaw's Division, 1st Corps, Army of Northern Virginia
(April-August 1864)

Humphreys' Brigade, Kershaw's Division, Valley District, Department of
Northern Virginia (August-October 1864)

Humphreys' Brigade, Kershaw's Division, 1st Corps, Army of Northern Virginia
(November 1864-April 1865)

**Battles:**   Blackburn's Ford (July 18, 1861)
1st Bull Run (July 21, 1861)
Edwards' Ferry (October 4, 1861)
Ball's Bluff (October 21, 1861)
Yorktown Siege (April-May 1862)
Warwick Road (April 5, 1862)
Lee's Mill (April 16, 1862)
Yorktown [detachment] (April 26, 1862)
Seven Pines (May 31-June 1, 1862)
Seven Days Battles (June 25-July 1, 1862)
Allen's Farm (June 29, 1862)
Savage's Station (June 29, 1862)
Malvern Hill (July 1, 1862)
Harpers Ferry (September 12-15, 1862)
Maryland Heights (September 13, 1862)
South Mountain (September 14, 1862)
Antietam (September 17, 1862)
Fredericksburg (December 13, 1862)
Chancellorsville (May 1-4, 1863)
Gettysburg (July 1-3, 1863)
Chickamauga (September 19-20, 1863)
Chattanooga Siege (September-November 1863)
Wauhatchie (October 28-29, 1863)
Knoxville Siege (November-December 1863)
Fort Sanders (November 29, 1863)

Dandridge (January 17, 1864)
Fair Garden (January 27, 1864)
The Wilderness (May 5-6, 1864)
Spotsylvania Court House (May 8-21, 1864)
North Anna (May 23-26, 1864)
Totopotomy River (May 30, 1864)
Cold Harbor (June 1-3, 1864)
Petersburg Siege (June 1864-April 1865)
Weldon Railroad (June 22, 1864)
Deep Bottom, Strawberry Plains, and New Market Road (July 27-29, 1864)
Malvern Hill (July 28, 1864)
Cedarville (August 16, 1864)
Front Royal (August 16, 1864)
Bunker Hill (September 2-3, 1864)
Berryville (September 4, 1864)
Cedar Creek (October 19, 1864)
Petersburg Siege (June 1864-April 1865)
Hatcher's Run (February 5-7, 1865)
Sayler's Creek (April 6, 1865)
Appomattox Court House (April 9, 1865)
**Further Reading:**   Cooper, Norman Lee and Sifakis, Stewart James, *A Confederate Soldier and His Descendants*. McNeily, J. S., *Barksdale's Mississippi Brigade at Gettysburg.*

## 177.   MISSISSIPPI 18TH INFANTRY REGIMENT

**Organization:**   Organized on June 7, 1861. Reorganized on April 26, 1862. Surrendered at Appomattox Court House, Virginia on April 9, 1865.
**First Commander:**   Erasmus R. Burt (Colonel)
**Field Officers:**   John W. Balfour (Major)
James C. Campbell (Major)
George B. Gerald (Major)
Thomas M. Griffin (Lieutenant Colonel, Colonel)
Eli G. Henry (Major)
Walter G. Kearney (Lieutenant Colonel)
William H. Luse (Lieutenant Colonel)
**Assignments:**   Department of Alexandria (June 1861)
D. R. Jones' Brigade, Army of the Potomac (June-July 1861)
D. R. Jones' Brigade, 1st Corps, Army of the Potomac (July 1861)
Evans' Brigade, 1st Corps, Army of the Potomac (July-October 1861)
Evans'-Griffith's Brigade, Forces at Leesburg [D. H. Hill's Division], Potomac District, Department of Northern Virginia (October 1861-March 1862)

Griffith's Brigade, McLaws'-Magruder's Division, Department of Northern Virginia (April-May 1862)

Griffith's-Barksdale's Brigade, Magruder's Division, Army of Northern Virginia (June-July 1862)

Barksdale's-Humphreys' Brigade, McLaws' Division, 1st Corps, Army of Northern Virginia (July 1862-September 1863)

Humphreys' Brigade, McLaws' Division, Longstreet's Corps, Army of Tennessee (September-November 1863)

Humphreys' Brigade, McLaws'-Kershaw's Division, Department of East Tennessee (November 1863-April 1864)

Humphreys' Brigade, Kershaw's Division, 1st Corps, Army of Northern Virginia (April-August 1864)

Humphreys' Brigade, Kershaw's Division, Valley District, Department of Northern Virginia (August-October 1864)

Humphreys' Brigade, Kershaw's Division, 1st Corps, Army of Northern Virginia (November 1864-April 1865)

**Battles:** Blackburn's Ford (July 18, 1861)

1st Bull Run (July 21, 1861)

Ball's Bluff (October 21, 1861)

Yorktown Siege (April-May 1862)

Warwick Road (April 5, 1862)

Yorktown [detachment] (April 26, 1862)

Seven Pines (May 31-June 1, 1862)

Seven Days Battles (June 25-July 1, 1862)

Allen's Farm (June 29, 1862)

Savage's Station (June 29, 1862)

Malvern Hill (July 1, 1862)

Harpers Ferry (September 12-15, 1862)

Maryland Heights (September 13, 1862)

South Mountain (September 14, 1862)

Antietam (September 17, 1862)

Fredericksburg (December 13, 1862)

Chancellorsville (May 1-4, 1863)

Gettysburg (July 1-3, 1863)

Chickamauga (September 19-20, 1863)

Chattanooga Siege (September-November 1863)

Wauhatchie (October 28-29, 1863)

Knoxville Siege (November-December 1863)

Fort Sanders (November 29, 1863)

Dandridge (January 17, 1864)

Fair Garden (January 27, 1864)

The Wilderness (May 5-6, 1864)
Spotsylvania Court House (May 8-21, 1864)
North Anna (May 23-26, 1864)
Totopotomy River (May 30, 1864)
Cold Harbor (June 1-3, 1864)
Petersburg Siege (June 1864-April 1865)
Weldon Railroad (June 22, 1864)
Deep Bottom, Strawberry Plains, and New Market Road (July 27-29, 1864)
Malvern Hill (July 28, 1864)
Cedarville (August 16, 1864)
Front Royal (August 16, 1864)
Bunker Hill (September 2-3, 1864)
Berryville (September 4, 1864)
Cedar Creek (October 19, 1864)
Petersburg Siege (June 1864-April 1865)
Hatcher's Run (February 5-7, 1865)
Sayler's Creek (April 6, 1865)
Appomattox Court House (April 9, 1865)
**Further Reading:**   McNeily, J. S., *Barksdale's Mississippi Brigade at Gettysburg.*
Dinkins, James, *1861-1865 by an "Old Johnny."*

## 178.   MISSISSIPPI 19TH INFANTRY REGIMENT

**Organization:**   Organized for the war on June 11, 1861. Surrendered at Appo-
mattox Court House, Virginia on April 9, 1865.
**First Commander:**   Christopher H. Mott (Colonel)
**Field Officers:**   Benjamin Allston (Major)
Robert A. Dean (Major)
James H. Duncan (Lieutenant Colonel)
Thomas J. Hardin (Major, Lieutenant Colonel, Colonel)
Nathaniel H. Harris (Major, Lieutenant Colonel, Colonel)
Lucius Q. C. Lamar (Lieutenant Colonel, Colonel)
John Mullins (Major, Lieutenant Colonel, Colonel)
Richard W. Phipps (Major, Lieutenant Colonel, Colonel)
Thomas R. Reading (Major)
Abner Smead (Major)
Ward G. Vaughan (Major, Lieutenant Colonel)
**Assignments:**   Forney's Brigade, Army of the Shenandoah (July 1861)
Forney's-Wilcox's Brigade, 2nd Corps, Army of the Potomac (July-October
    1861)
Wilcox's Brigade, 2nd Corps, Potomac District, Department of Northern
    Virginia (October 1861-January 1862)

Wilcox's Brigade, G. W. Smith's Division, Potomac District, Department of Northern Virginia (January-March 1862)

Wilcox's Brigade, Longstreet's Division, Army of Northern Virginia (March-June 1862)

Featherston's Brigade, Longstreet's Division, Army of Northern Virginia (June 1862)

Featherston's Brigade, Longstreet's Division, 1st Corps, Army of Northern Virginia (June-August 1862)

Featherston's Brigade, Wilcox's Division, 1st Corps, Army of Northern Virginia (August-September 1862)

Featherston's-Posey's Brigade, R. H. Anderson's Division, 1st Corps, Army of Northern Virginia (September 1862-May 1863)

Posey's-Harris' Brigade, R. H. Anderson's-Mahone's Division, 3rd Corps, Army of Northern Virginia (May 1863-April 1865)

**Battles:** Yorktown Siege (April-May 1862)

Lee's Mill (April 16, 1862)

Seven Pines (May 31-June 1, 1862)

Seven Days Battles (June 25-July 1, 1862)

Gaines' Mill (June 27, 1862)

Frayser's Farm (June 30, 1862)

2nd Bull Run (August 28-30, 1862)

Antietam (September 17, 1862)

Fredericksburg (December 13, 1862)

Chancellorsville (May 1-4, 1863)

Gettysburg (July 1-3, 1863)

Bristoe Campaign (October 1863)

Mine Run Campaign (November-December 1863)

The Wilderness (May 5-6, 1864)

Spotsylvania Court House (May 8-21, 1864)

North Anna (May 23-26, 1864)

Cold Harbor (June 1-3, 1864)

Petersburg Siege (June 1864-April 1865)

Appomattox Court House (April 9, 1865)

**Further Reading:** Dinkins, James, *1861-1865 by an "Old Johnny."*

## 179.  MISSISSIPPI 20TH INFANTRY BATTALION, SHARPSHOOTERS

*See:* MISSISSIPPI 1ST INFANTRY BATTALION, SHARPSHOOTERS

## 180.  MISSISSIPPI 20TH INFANTRY REGIMENT

*Organization:*  Organized in the spring of 1861. Mustered into Confederate service for the war in June 1861. Surrendered at Fort Donelson on February 16, 1862. Exchanged in April 1862. Consolidated Consolidated with the 6th, 15th, and 23rd Infantry Regiments and designated as the 15th Infantry Regiment Consolidated at Smithfield, North Carolina on April 9, 1865.

*First Commander:*  Daniel R. Russell (Colonel)

*Field Officers:*  William N. Brown (Major, Lieutenant Colonel, Colonel)
William M. Chatfield (Major)
Thomas B. Graham (Major)
Conrad K. Massey (Major)
Horace H. Miller (Lieutenant Colonel)
Walter A. Rorer (Major, Lieutenant Colonel)

*Assignments:*  Army of the Kanawha (September-October 1861)
Floyd's Brigade, Department of Northern Virginia (October 1861-January 1862)
Floyd's Division, Central Army of Kentucky, Department #2 (January-February 1862)
McCausland's Brigade, Floyd's Division, Fort Donelson, Department #2 (February 1862)
3rd Sub-district, District of the Mississippi, Department #2 (July-August 1862)
Baldwin's Brigade, Tilghman's Division, 1st Corps, Department of Mississippi and East Louisiana (October 1862-January 1863)
Tilghman's Brigade, Loring's Division, Army of North Mississippi, Department of Mississippi and East Louisiana (January-February 1863)
Tilghman's Brigade, Loring's Division, 2nd Military District, Department of Mississippi and East Louisiana (March-April 1863)
4th Military District, Department of Mississippi and East Louisiana (April-May 1863)
Tilghman's Brigade, Loring's Division, Department of Mississippi and East Louisiana (May 1863)
Tilghman's-Reynolds'-Adams' Brigade, Loring's Division, Department of the West (May-July 1863)
Adams' Brigade, Loring's Division, Department of Mississippi and East Louisiana (July 1863-January 1864)
Adams' Brigade, Loring's Division, Department of Alabama, Mississippi, and East Louisiana (January-May 1864)
Adams' Brigade, Loring's Division, Army of Mississippi (May-July 1864)
Adams' Brigade, Loring's Division, 3rd Corps, Army of Tennessee (July 1864-April 1865)

*Battles:*  Fort Donelson (February 12-16, 1862)

Fort Pemberton (March 11, 1863)
Fort Pemberton (March 13, 1863)
Fort Pemberton (March 16, 1863)
Fort Pemberton (April 2, 1863)
Fort Pemberton (April 4, 1863)
Vicksburg Campaign (May-July 1863)
Champion Hill (May 16, 1863)
Jackson Siege (July 1863)
Meridian Campaign (February-March 1864)
Atlanta Campaign (May-September 1864)
New Hope Church (May 25-June 4, 1864)
Peach Tree Creek (July 20, 1864)
Ezra Church (July 28, 1864)
Atlanta Siege (July-September 1864)
Jonesboro (August 31-September 1, 1864)
Franklin (November 30, 1864)
Nashville (December 15-16, 1864)
Carolinas Campaign (February-April 1865)
Bentonville (March 19-21, 1865)

## 181. MISSISSIPPI 21ST INFANTRY REGIMENT

*Organization:*  Organized for the war in mid-1861. Surrendered at Appomattox Court House, Virginia on April 9, 1865.
*First Commander:*  Benjamin G. Humphreys (Colonel)
*Field Officers:*  William L. Brandon (Lieutenant Colonel, Colonel)
William H. Fitzgerald (Major, Lieutenant Colonel)
Daniel N. Moody (Major, Lieutenant Colonel, Colonel)
John Sims (Major, Lieutenant Colonel)
John G. Taylor (Major)
*Assignments:*  Griffith's Brigade, Forces at Leesburg [D. H. Hill's Division], Potomac District, Department of Northern Virginia (January-March 1862)
Griffith's Brigade, McLaws'-Magruder's Division, Department of Northern Virginia (April-May 1862)
Griffith's-Barksdale's Brigade, Magruder's Division, Army of Northern Virginia (June-July 1862)
Barksdale's-Humphreys' Brigade, McLaws' Division, 1st Corps, Army of Northern Virginia (July 1862-September 1863)
Humphreys' Brigade, McLaws' Division, Longstreet's Corps, Army of Tennessee (September-November 1863)
Humphreys' Brigade, McLaws'-Kershaw's Division, Department of East Tennessee (November 1863-April 1864)

Humphreys' Brigade, Kershaw's Division, 1st Corps, Army of Northern Virginia (April-August 1864)

Humphreys' Brigade, Kershaw's Division, Valley District, Department of Northern Virginia (August-October 1864)

Humphreys' Brigade, Kershaw's Division, 1st Corps, Army of Northern Virginia (November 1864-April 1865)

**Battles:**  Yorktown Siege (April-May 1862)

Seven Pines (May 31-June 1, 1862)

Seven Days Battles (June 25-July 1, 1862)

Allen's Farm (June 29, 1862)

Savage's Station (June 29, 1862)

Malvern Hill (July 1, 1862)

Harpers Ferry (September 12-15, 1862)

Maryland Heights (September 13, 1862)

South Mountain (September 14, 1862)

Antietam (September 17, 1862)

Fredericksburg (December 13, 1862)

Chancellorsville (May 1-4, 1863)

Gettysburg (July 1-3, 1863)

Chickamauga (September 19-20, 1863)

Chattanooga Siege (September-November 1863)

Wauhatchie (October 28-29, 1863)

Knoxville Siege (November 1863)

Fort Sanders (November 29, 1863)

Dandridge (January 17, 1864)

Fair Garden (January 27, 1864)

The Wilderness (May 5-6, 1864)

Spotsylvania Court House (May 8-21, 1864)

North Anna (May 23-26, 1864)

Totopotomy River (May 30, 1864)

Cold Harbor (June 1-3, 1864)

Petersburg Siege (June 1864-April 1865)

Weldon Railroad (June 22, 1864)

Deep Bottom, Strawberry Plains, and New Market Road (July 27-29, 1864)

Malvern Hill (July 28, 1864)

Cedarville (August 16, 1864)

Front Royal (August 16, 1864)

Bunker Hill (September 2-3, 1864)

Berryville (September 4, 1864)

Cedar Creek (October 19, 1864)

Petersburg Siege (June 1864-April 1865)

Hatcher's Run (February 5-7, 1865)
Sayler's Creek (April 6, 1865)
Appomattox Court House (April 9, 1865)
**Further Reading:** McNeily, J. S., *Barksdale's Mississippi Brigade at Gettysburg*.
Dinkins, James, *1861-1865 by an "Old Johnny"*.

## 182. MISSISSIPPI 22ND INFANTRY REGIMENT

*Organization:* Organized in mid-1861. Mustered into Confederate service for
the war in mid-1861. Consolidated with the 1st Sharpshooters Battalion, and
the 1st and 33rd Infantry Regiments and designated as the 22nd Infantry
Regiment Consolidated at Smithfield, North Carolina on April 9, 1865.
*First Commander:* D. W. C. Bonham (Colonel)
*Field Officers:* Thomas C. Dockery (Major)
James D. Lester (Colonel)
Charles G. Nelms (Major, Lieutenant Colonel)
Martin A. Oatis (Major)
James S. Prestidge (Major, Lieutenant Colonel)
Frank Schaller (Lieutenant Colonel, Colonel)
*Assignments:* Bowen's Brigade, 1st Geographical Division, Department #2
(September-October 1861)
Bonham's Brigade, Bowen's Division, 1st Geographical Division, Department
#2 (October-November 1861)
1st Brigade, Bowen's Division, 1st Geographical Division, Department #2
(November-December 1861)
1st Brigade, Bowen's Division, Central Army of Kentucky, Department #2
(December 1861-January 1862)
Bowen's Brigade, Central Army of Kentucky, Department #2 (January-February 1862)
Staham's Brigade, Crittenden's Division, Central Army of Kentucky, Department #2 (February-March 1862)
Statham's Brigade, Reserve Corps, Army of the Mississippi, Department #2
(March-June 1862)
Statham's Brigade, Breckinridge's Division, Department of Southern Mississippi and East Louisiana (June-July 1862)
Statham's-Smith's Brigade, Breckinridge's Division, District of the Mississippi,
Department #2 (July 1862)
Smith's Brigade, Clark's Division, Breckinridge's Command, District of the
Mississippi, Department #2 (July-August 1862)
Bowen's Brigade, Lovell's Division, District of the Mississippi, Department #2
(September-October 1862)

Thompson's Brigade, Rust's Division, Department of Mississippi and East Louisiana (October-December 1862)

Thompson's Brigade, Rust's Division, 1st Corps, Army of North Mississippi, Department of Mississippi and East Louisiana (December 1862-January 1863)

Rust's-Featherston's Brigade, Loring's Division, Army of North Mississippi, Department of Mississippi and East Louisiana (January-February 1863)

Featherston's Brigade, Loring's Division, 5th Military District, Department of Mississippi and East Louisiana (March-April 1863)

Featherston's Brigade, Loring's Division, Department of Mississippi and East Louisiana (April-May 1863)

Featherston's Brigade, Loring's Division, Department of the West (May-July 1863)

Featherston's Brigade, Loring's Division, Department of Mississippi and East Louisiana (July 1863-January 1864)

Featherston's Brigade, Loring's Division, Department of Alabama, Mississippi, and East Louisiana (January-May 1864)

Featherston's Brigade, Loring's Division, Army of Mississippi (May-July 1864)

Featherston's Brigade, Loring's Division, 3rd Corps, Army of Tennessee (July 1864-April 1865)

**Battles:**  Shiloh (April 6-7, 1862)

Vicksburg Bombardments (May 18-July 27, 1862)

Baton Rouge (August 5, 1862)

Rolling Fork (March 20, 1863)

Fore's Plantation (March 25, 1863)

Vicksburg Campaign (May-July 1863)

Champion Hill (May 16, 1863)

Jackson Siege (July 1863)

Meridian Campaign (February-March 1864)

Atlanta Campaign (May-September 1864)

New Hope Church (May 25-June 4, 1864)

Peach Tree Creek (July 20, 1864)

Ezra Church (July 28, 1864)

Atlanta Siege (July-September 1864)

Jonesboro (August 31-September 1, 1864)

Franklin (November 30, 1864)

Nashville (December 15-16, 1864)

Carolinas Campaign (February-April 1865)

Bentonville (March 19-21, 1865)

## 183. MISSISSIPPI 22ND INFANTRY REGIMENT, CONSOLIDATED

*Organization:* Organized by the consolidation of the 1st Sharpshooters Battalion and the 1st, 22nd, and 33rd Infantry Regiments at Smithfield, North Carolina on April 9, 1865. Surrendered by General Joseph E. Johnston at Durham Station, Orange County, North Carolina on April 26, 1865.

*First Commander:* Martin A. Otis (Colonel)

*Assignment:* Featherston's Brigade, Loring's Division, 3rd Corps, Army of Tennessee (April 1865)

*Battle:* Carolinas Campaign (February-April 1865)

## 184. MISSISSIPPI 23RD INFANTRY REGIMENT

*Also Known As:* 2nd Infantry Regiment

3rd Infantry Regiment

*Organization:* Organized as the 2nd Infantry Regiment in mid-1861. Designated as the 23rd Infantry Regiment on November 19, 1861. Surrendered at Fort Donelson on February 16, 1862. Consolidated with the 6th, 15th, and 20th Infantry Regiments and designated as the 15th Infantry Regiment Consolidated at Smithfield, North Carolina on April 9, 1865.

*First Commander:* Thomas J. Davidson (Colonel)

*Field Officers:* John R. Duvall (Major)

George W. B. Garnett (Major)

Moses McCarley (Lieutenant Colonel)

W. E. Rogers (Major)

Joseph M. Wells (Lieutenant Colonel, Colonel)

*Assignments:* Davidson's Brigade, Johnson's Division, Fort Donelson, Department #2 (February 1862)

Baldwin's Brigade, Tilghman's Division, 1st Corps, Army of West Tennessee, Department of Mississippi and East Louisiana (December 1862)

Baldwin's Brigade, Tilghman's Division, 1st Corps, Army of North Mississippi, Department of Mississippi and East Louisiana (December 1862-January 1863)

Tilghman's Brigade, Loring's Division, Army of North Mississippi, Department of Mississippi and East Louisiana (January-February 1863)

Tilghman's Brigade, Loring's Division, 2nd Military District, Department of Mississippi and East Louisiana (March-April 1863)

4th Military District, Department of Mississippi and East Louisiana (April-May 1863)

Tilghman's Brigade, Loring's Division, Department of Mississippi and East Louisiana (May 1863)

Tilghman's-Reynolds'-Adams' Brigade, Loring's Division, Department of the West (May-July 1863)

Adams' Brigade, Loring's Division, Department of Mississippi and East Louisiana (July 1863-January 1864)

Adams' Brigade, Loring's Division, Department of Alabama, Mississippi, and East Louisiana (January-May 1864)

Adams' Brigade, Loring's Division, Army of Mississippi (May-July 1864)

Adams' Brigade, Loring's Division, 3rd Corps, Army of Tennessee (July 1864-April 1865)

**Battles:**   Fort Donelson (February 12-16, 1862)

Coffeeville (December 5, 1862)

Rolling Fork (March 20, 1863)

Fore's Plantation (March 25, 1863)

Vicksburg Campaign (May-July 1863)

Champion Hill (May 16, 1863)

Jackson Siege (July 1863)

Atlanta Campaign (May-September 1864)

New Hope Church (May 25-June 4, 1864)

Peach Tree Creek (July 20, 1864)

Ezra Church (July 28, 1864)

Atlanta Siege (July-September 1864)

Jonesboro (August 31-September 1, 1864)

Franklin (November 30, 1864)

Nashville (December 15-16, 1864)

Carolinas Campaign (February-April 1865)

Bentonville (March 19-21, 1865)

## 185.  MISSISSIPPI 24TH INFANTRY REGIMENT

**Organization:**   Organized in mid-1861. Mustered into Confederate service for the war in mid-1861. Field consolidation with the 27th Infantry Regiment from October 1863 to August 1864. Field consolidation with the 27th and 34th Infantry Regiments in September 1864. Field consolidation with the 34th Infantry Regiment from December 1864 to April 9, 1865. Additional field consolidation with the 27th Infantry Regiment in early 1865. Consolidated with the 27th, 29th, 30th, and 34th Infantry Regiments and designated as the 24th Infantry Regiment Consolidated at Smithfield, North Carolina on April 9, 1865.

**First Commander:**   William F. Dowd (Colonel)

**Field Officers:**   Clifton Dancy (Lieutenant Colonel)

George M. Govan (Major)

William L. Lyles (Lieutenant Colonel)

Robert P. McKelvaine (Lieutenant Colonel, Colonel)

William C. Staples (Major)

R. W. Williamson (Colonel)

*Assignments:* Department of Middle and Eastern Florida (December 1861-March 1862)

Maxey's Brigade, Department of East Tennessee (April 1862)

Detached (Maxey's) Brigade, 1st Corps, Army of the Mississippi, Department #2 (May-July 1862)

Maxey's Brigade, Cheatham's Division, Army of the Mississippi, Department #2 (July 1862)

Maxey's Brigade, Cheatham's Division, Army of the Mississippi, Department #2 (July-August 1862)

Powel's Brigade, Anderson's Division, 2nd Corps, Army of Tennessee (November-December 1862)

Anderson's-Walthall's Brigade, Withers'-Hindman's Division, 1st Corps, Army of Tennessee (December 1862-September 1863)

Walthall's Brigade, Liddell's Division, Reserve Corps, Army of Tennessee (September 1863)

Walthall's Brigade, Hindman's Division, 1st Corps, Army of Tennessee (September 1862-November 1863)

Walthall's Brigade, Cheatham's Division, 1st Corps, Army of Tennessee (November 1863-February 1864)

Walthall's-Brantley's Brigade, Hindman's-Anderson's-Johnson's-D. H. Hill's Division, 2nd Corps, Army of Tennessee (February 1864-April 1865)

*Battles:* Murfreesboro (December 31, 1862-January 3, 1863)

Tullahoma Campaign (June 1863)

Chickamauga (September 19-20, 1863)

Chattanooga Siege (September-November 1863)

Chattanooga (November 23-25, 1863)

Atlanta Campaign (May-September 1864)

Resaca (May 14-15, 1864)

New Hope Church (May 25-June 4, 1864)

Ezra Church (July 28, 1864)

Atlanta Siege (July-September 1864)

Franklin (November 30, 1864)

Nashville (December 15-16, 1864)

Carolinas Campaign (February-April 1865)

*Further Reading:* Dennis, Frank, *Kemper County Rebel: The Civil War Diary of Robert Masten Holmes, C.S.A..*

## 186. MISSISSIPPI 24TH INFANTRY REGIMENT, CONSOLIDATED

*Organization:* Organized by the consolidation of the 24th, 27th, 29th, 30th, and 34th Infantry Regiments at Smithfield, North Carolina on April 9, 1865.

Surrendered by General Joseph E. Johnston at Durham Station, Orange County, North Carolina on April 26, 1865.

**First Commander:** R. W. Williamson (Colonel)

**Assignment:** Brantley's Brigade, D. H. Hill's Division, 2nd Corps, Army of Tennessee (April 1865)

**Battle:** Carolinas Campaign (February-April 1865)

## 187. MISSISSIPPI 25TH INFANTRY REGIMENT

**Organization:** Organized with three Mississippi, two Alabama, one Kentucky, one South Carolina, one Arkansas, and two Missouri companies in mid-1861. Designated as the 2nd Confederate Infantry Regiment on January 31, 1862.

**First Commander:** John D. Martin (Colonel)

**Field Officers:** Edward F. McGehee (Lieutenant Colonel)

Thomas H. Mangham (Major)

**Assignments:** Bowen's Brigade, 1st Geographical Division, Department #2 (October 1861)

Martin's Brigade, Bowen's Division, 1st Geographical Division, Department #2 (October 1861)

2nd Brigade, Bowen's Division, 1st Geographical Division, Department #2 (November-December 1861)

Bowen's Brigade, Central Army of Kentucky, Department #2 (December 1861-January 1862)

Bowen's Brigade, Central Army of Kentucky, Department #2 (January 1862)

## 188. MISSISSIPPI 26TH INFANTRY REGIMENT

**Organization:** Organized for the war on September 10, 1861. Surrendered at Fort Donelson on February 16, 1862. Surrendered at Appomattox Court House, Virginia on April 9, 1865.

**First Commander:** Arthur E. Reynolds (Colonel)

**Field Officers:** Francis M. Boone (Lieutenant Colonel)

Tully F. Parker (Major)

**Assignments:** Baldwin's Brigade, Buckner's Division, 1st Geographical Division, Department #2 (December 1861)

Baldwin's Brigade, Buckner's Division, Central Army of Kentucky, Department #2 (January-February 1862)

Baldwin's Brigade, Buckner's Division, Fort Donelson, Department #2 (February 1862)

Baldwin's Brigade, Tilghman's Division, 1st Corps, Army of West Tennessee, Department of Mississippi and East Louisiana (December 1862)

Baldwin's Brigade, Tilghman's Division, 1st Corps, Army of the Department of Mississippi and East Louisiana (December 1862-January 1863)

Tilghman's Brigade, Loring's Division, 5th Military District, Army of the Department of Mississippi and East Louisiana (January 1863)

Tilghman's Brigade, Loring's Division, Department of Mississippi and East Louisiana (January-February 1863)

Tilghman's Brigade, Loring's Division, 5th Military District, Department of Mississippi and East Louisiana (April 1863)

Tilghman's Brigade, Loring's Division, Department of Mississippi and East Louisiana (April-May 1863)

Tilghman's-J. Adams' Brigade, Loring's Division, Department of the West (May-July 1863)

J. Adams' Brigade, Loring's Division, Department of Mississippi and East Louisiana (July 1863-March 1864)

Davis' Brigade, Heth's Division, 3rd Corps, Army of Northern Virginia (March 1864-April 1865)

**Battles:**   Fort Donelson (February 12-16, 1862)
Coffeeville (December 5, 1862)
Fort Pemberton (March 11, 1863)
Fort Pemberton (March 13, 1863)
Fort Pemberton (March 16, 1863)
Fort Pemberton (April 2, 1863)
Fort Pemberton (April 4, 1863)
Vicksburg Campaign (May-July 1863)
Champion Hill (May 16, 1863)
Jackson Siege (July 1863)
Meridian Campaign (February-March 1864)
The Wilderness (May 5-6, 1864)
Spotsylvania Court House (May 8-21, 1864)
North Anna (May 23-26, 1864)
Bethesda Church (May 31, 1864)
Cold Harbor (June 1-3, 1864)
Petersburg Siege (June 1864-April 1865)
Weldon Railroad (August 18-22, 1864)
Hatcher's Run (February 5-7, 1865)
Appomattox Court House (April 9, 1865)

## 189. MISSISSIPPI 27TH INFANTRY REGIMENT

**Organization:**   Organized in September 1861. Field consolidation with the 24th Infantry Regiment from October 1863 to August 1864. Field consolidation with the 24th and 34th Infantry Regiments from September 1864 to April 9, 1865. Consolidated with the 24th, 29th, 30th, and 34th Infantry Regiments at Smithfield, North Carolina on April 9, 1865.

*First Commander:*   Thomas M. Jones (Colonel)
*Field Officers:*   James L. Autry (Lieutenant Colonel)
James A. Campbell (Major, Lieutenant Colonel, Colonel)
Andrew J. Hays (Lieutenant Colonel)
Andrew J. Jones (Lieutenant Colonel)
Julius B. Kennedy (Major)
George H. Lipscomb (Major)
Amos McLemore (Major)
*Assignments:*   Army of Pensacola, Department of Alabama and West Florida (January-March 1862)
Department of Alabama and West Florida (March-June 1862)
District of the Gulf, Department #2 (July 1862)
Jackson's Brigade, Withers' Division, Army of the Mississippi, Department #2 (July-August 1862)
Jackson's Brigade, Withers' Division, Right Wing, Army of the Mississippi, Department #2 (August 1862)
Jones' Brigade, Anderson's Division, Left Wing, Army of the Mississippi, Department #2 (August-November 1862)
Jones' Brigade, Anderson's Division, 2nd Corps, Army of Tennessee (November-December 1862)
Anderson's-Walthall's Brigade, Withers'-Hindman's Division, 1st Corps, Army of Tennessee (December 1862-September 1863)
Walthall's Brigade, Liddell's Division, Reserve Corps, Army of Tennessee (September 1863)
Walthall's Brigade, Hindman's Division, 1st Corps, Army of Tennessee (September-November 1863)
Walthall's-Brigade, Cheatham's Division, 1st Corps, Army of Tennessee (November 1863-February 1864)
Walthall's-Brantley's Brigade, Hindman's-Anderson's-Johnson's-D. H. Hill's Division, 2nd Corps, Army of Tennessee (February 1864-April 1865)
*Battles:*   Pensacola (September 1861-January 1862)
Perryville (October 8, 1862)
Murfreesboro (December 31, 1862-January 3, 1863)
Tullahoma Campaign (June 1863)
Chickamauga (September 19-20, 1863)
Chattanooga Siege (September-November 1863)
Chattanooga (November 23-25, 1863)
Atlanta Campaign (May-September 1864)
Resaca (May 14-15, 1864)
New Hope Church (May 25-June 4, 1864)
Ezra Church (July 28, 1864)

Atlanta Siege (July-September 1864)
Franklin (November 30, 1864)
Nashville (December 15-16, 1864)
Carolinas Campaign (February-April 1865)

## 190. MISSISSIPPI 28TH INFANTRY REGIMENT
*See:* MISSISSIPPI 28TH CAVALRY REGIMENT

## 191. MISSISSIPPI 29TH INFANTRY REGIMENT

**Organization:** Organized ca. April 11, 1862. Field consolidation with the 30th Infantry Regiment from October 1863 to November 1863. Field consolidation with the 30th and 34th Infantry Regiments from December 1863 to May 1864. Field consolidation with the 30th Infantry Regiment from May 1864 to April 9, 1865. Consolidated with the 24th, 27th, 30th, and 34th Infantry Regiments and designated as the 24th Infantry Regiment Consolidated at Smithfield, North Carolina on April 9, 1865.
**First Commander:** Edward C. Walthall (Colonel)
**Field Officers:** William F. Brantley (Lieutenant Colonel, Colonel)
Newton A. Isom (Major)
James B. Morgan (Major, Lieutenant Colonel)
George W. Reynolds (Major)
**Assignments:** Chalmers' Brigade, Withers' Division, 1st Corps, Army of the Mississippi, Department #2 (June 1862)
Chalmers' Brigade, Reserve Corps, Army of the Mississippi, Department #2 (June-July 1862)
Chalmers' Brigade, Withers' Division, Army of the Mississippi, Department #2 (July-August 1862)
Chalmers' Brigade, Withers' Division, Right Wing, Army of the Mississippi, Department #2 (August-November 1862)
Chalmers' Brigade, Withers' Division, 1st Corps, Army of Tennessee (November-December 1862)
Anderson's-Walthall's Brigade, Withers'-Hindman's Division, 1st Corps, Army of Tennessee (December 1862-September 1863)
Walthall's Brigade, Liddell's Division, Reserve Corps, Army of Tennessee (September 1863)
Walthall's Brigade, Hindman's Division, 1st Corps, Army of Tennessee (September-November 1863)
Walthall's Brigade, Cheatham's Division, 1st Corps, Army of Tennessee (November 1863-February 1864)
Walthall's-Brantley's Brigade, Hindman's-Anderson's-Johnson's-D. H. Hill's Division, 2nd Corps, Army of Northern Virginia (February 1864-April 1865)

**Battles:**   Kentucky Campaign (August-October 1862)
Munfordville (September 17, 1862)
Murfreesboro (December 31, 1862-January 3, 1863)
Tullahoma Campaign (June 1863)
Chickamauga (September 19-20, 1863)
Chattanooga Siege (September-November 1863)
Chattanooga (November 23-25, 1863)
Atlanta Campaign (May-September 1864)
Resaca (May 14-15, 1864)
Cassville (May 19-22, 1864)
New Hope Church (May 25-June 4, 1864)
Ezra Church (July 28, 1864)
Atlanta Siege (July-September 1864)
Franklin (November 30, 1864)
Nashville (December 15-16, 1864)
Carolinas Campaign (February-April 1865)
**Further Reading:**   Robuck, J. E., *My Own Personal Experiences as a Soldier in the Confederate Army During the Civil War, 1861-1865.*

## 192.  MISSISSIPPI 30TH INFANTRY REGIMENT

**Organization:**   Organized in the spring of 1862. Field consolidation with the 29th Infantry Regiment from October 1863 to November 1863. Field consolidation with the 29th and 34th Infantry Regiments from December 1863 to May 1864. Field consolidation with the 29th Infantry Regiment from May 1864 to April 9, 1865. Consolidated with the 24th, 27th, 29th, and 34th Infantry Regiments and designated as the 24th Infantry Regiment. Consolidated at Smithfield, North Carolina on April 9, 1865.
**First Commander:**   George G.F. Neill (Colonel)
**Field Officers:**   John K. Allen (Major)
James M. Johnson (Major, Lieutenant Colonel)
Hugh A. Reynolds (Major, Lieutenant Colonel)
Junius I. Scales (Lieutenant Colonel, Colonel)
**Assignments:**   Anderson's Brigade, 2nd Corps, Army of the Mississippi, Department #2 (June-July 1862)
Anderson's Brigade, Jones' Division, Army of the Mississippi, Department #2 (July 1862)
T. M. Jones' Brigade, Jones'-Anderson's Division, Left Wing, Army of the Mississippi, Department #2 (October-November 1862)
T. M. Jones' Brigade, Anderson's Division, 1st Corps, Army of Tennessee (November-December 1862)

Anderson's-Walthall's Brigade, Withers'-Hindman's Division, 1st Corps, Army of Tennessee (December 1862-September 1863)

Walthall's Brigade, Liddell's Division, Reserve Corps, Army of Tennessee (September 1863)

Walthall's Brigade, Hindman's Division, 1st Corps, Army of Tennessee (September-November 1863)

Walthall's Brigade, Cheatham's Division, 1st Corps, Army of Tennessee (November 1863-February 1864)

Walthall's-Brantley's Brigade, Hindman's-Anderson's-Johnson's-D. H. Hill's Division, 2nd Corps, Army of Northern Virginia (February 1864-April 1865)

**Battles:** Perryville (October 8, 1862)

Murfreesboro (December 31, 1862-January 3, 1863)

Tullahoma Campaign (June 1863)

Chickamauga (September 19-20, 1863)

Chattanooga Siege (September-November 1863)

Chattanooga (November 23-25, 1863)

Atlanta Campaign (May-September 1864)

Resaca (May 14-15, 1864)

Cassville (May 19-22, 1864)

New Hope Church (May 25-June 4, 1864)

Ezra Church (July 28, 1864)

Atlanta Siege (July-September 1864)

Franklin (November 30, 1864)

Nashville (December 15-16, 1864)

Carolinas Campaign (February-April 1865)

## 193. MISSISSIPPI 31ST INFANTRY REGIMENT

**Organization:** Organized by the increase of the 5th Infantry Battalion to a regiment in early 1862. Consolidated with the 3rd and 40th Infantry Regiments and designated as the 3rd Infantry Regiment Consolidated at Smithfield, North Carolina on April 9, 1865.

**First Commander:** Jehu A. Orr (Colonel)

**Field Officers:** James W. Drane (Major, Lieutenant Colonel)

Francis M. Gillespie (Major)

Marcus D. L. Stephens (Lieutenant Colonel, Colonel)

Harvey E. Topp (Major)

**Assignments:** Helm's Brigade, Clark's Division, Breckinridge's Command, District of the Mississippi, Department #2 (August 1862)

Helm's Brigade, District of the Mississippi, Department #2 (September-October 1862)

Helm's Brigade, Department of Mississippi and East Louisiana (October 1862)

Thompson's Brigade, Rust's Division, 1st Corps, Army of North Mississippi, Department of Mississippi and East Louisiana (December 1862-January 1863)

Rust's Brigade, Loring's Division, Department of Mississippi and East Louisiana (January-February 1863)

Featherston's Brigade, Loring's Division, 2nd Military District, Department of Mississippi and East Louisiana (March-April 1863)

Featherston's Brigade, Loring's Division, Department of Mississippi and East Louisiana (April-May 1863)

Featherston's Brigade, Loring's Division, Department of the West (May-July 1863)

Featherston's Division, Loring's Division, Department of Mississippi and East Louisiana (July 1863-January 1864)

Featherston's Brigade, Loring's Division, Department of Alabama, Mississippi, and East Louisiana (January-May 1864)

Featherston's Brigade, Loring's Division, Army of Mississippi (May-July 1864)

Featherston's Brigade, Loring's Division, 3rd Corps, Army of Tennessee (July 1864-April 1865)

**Battles:**   Vicksburg Bombardments (May 18-July 27, 1862)

Baton Rouge (August 5, 1862)

Fore's Plantation (March 25, 1863)

Vicksburg Campaign (May-July 1863)

Champion Hill (May 16, 1863)

Jackson Siege (July 1863)

Meridian Campaign (February-March 1864)

Atlanta Campaign (May-September 1864)

New Hope Church (May 25-June 4, 1864)

Peach Tree Creek (July 20, 1864)

Ezra Church (July 28, 1864)

Atlanta Siege (July-September 1864)

Franklin (November 30, 1864)

Jonesboro (August 31-September 1, 1864)

Nashville (December 15-16, 1864)

Carolinas Campaign (February-April 1865)

## 194.   MISSISSIPPI 32ND INFANTRY REGIMENT

*Organization:*   Organized ca. April 3, 1862. Field consolidation with the 45th Infantry Regiment from July 1863 to early 1864. Field consolidation with the 8th Infantry Regiment from August 1864 to April 9, 1865. Consolidated with the 3rd (Williams') Infantry Battalion, the 8th Infantry Regiment, and part of the 5th Infantry Regiment and designated as the 8th Infantry Battalion. Consolidated at Smithfield, North Carolina on April 9, 1865.

**First Commander:** Mark P. Lowrey (Colonel)

**Field Officers:** F. C. Karr (Major)

J. W. Swinney (Major)

William H. H. Tison (Lieutenant Colonel, Colonel)

**Assignments:** Unattached, Army of the Mississippi, Department #2 (April-May 1862)

Wood's Brigade, 3rd Corps, Army of the Mississippi, Department #2 (June-July 1862)

Wood's Brigade, Hardee's Division, Army of the Mississippi, Department #2 (July-August 1862)

Wood's Brigade, Hardee's-Buckner's Division, Left Wing, Army of the Mississippi, Department #2 (August-November 1862)

Wood's-Lowrey's Brigade, Buckner's-Cleburne's Division, 2nd Corps, Army of Tennessee (November 1862-November 1863)

Lowrey's Brigade, Cleburne's Division, 1st Corps, Army of Tennessee (November 1863-April 1865)

**Battles:** Corinth Campaign (April-June 1862)

Tullahoma Campaign (June 1863)

Chickamauga (September 19-20, 1863)

Chattanooga Siege (September-November 1863)

Chattanooga (November 23-25, 1863)

Atlanta Campaign (May-September 1864)

New Hope Church (May 25-June 4, 1864)

Kennesaw Mountain (June 27, 1864)

Atlanta Siege (July-September 1864)

Atlanta (July 22, 1864)

Jonesboro (August 31-September 1, 1864)

Franklin (November 30, 1864)

Nashville (December 15-16, 1864)

Carolinas Campaign (February-April 1865)

## 195.  MISSISSIPPI 33RD (HARDCASTLE'S) INFANTRY REGIMENT

*See:* MISSISSIPPI 45TH INFANTRY REGIMENT

## 196.  MISSISSIPPI 33RD (HURST'S-DRAKE'S) INFANTRY REGIMENT

**Organization:** Organized in early 1862. Consolidated with the 1st Sharpshooters Battalion, and the 1st and 22nd Infantry Regiments and designated as the 22nd Infantry Regiment. Consolidated at Smithfield, North Carolina on April 9, 1865.

**First Commander:**  David W. Hurst (Colonel)

**Field Officers:**  Jabez L. Drake (Major, Lieutenant Colonel, Colonel)

Robert J. Hall (Major)

John Harrod (Major)

William B. Johnson (Lieutenant Colonel)

Charles P. Neilson (Lieutenant Colonel)

**Assignments:**  Grenada, Mississippi, Department #2 (June 1862)

3rd Sub-district, District of the Mississippi, Department #2 (July-August 1862)

Villepigue's Brigade, Lovell's Division, District of the Mississippi, Department #2 (October 1862)

Villepigue's Brigade, Lovell's Division, Department of Mississippi and East Louisiana (October-December 1862)

Scott's Brigade, Rust's Division, 1st Corps, Army of North Mississippi, Department of Mississippi and East Louisiana (December 1862-January 1863)

Rust's-Featherston's Brigade, Loring's Division, Army of North Mississippi, Department of Mississippi and East Louisiana (January-February 1863)

Featherston's Brigade, Loring's Division, 2nd Military District, Department of Mississippi and East Louisiana (March-April 1863)

Featherston's Brigade, Loring's Division, Department of Mississippi and East Louisiana (April-May 1863)

Featherston's Brigade, Loring's Division, Department of the West (May-July 1863)

Featherston's Brigade, Loring's Division, Department of Mississippi and East Louisiana (July 1863-January 1864)

Featherston's Brigade, Loring's Division, Department of Alabama, Mississippi, and East Louisiana (January-May 1864)

Featherston's Brigade, Loring's Division, Army of Mississippi (May-July 1864)

Featherston's Brigade, Loring's Division, 3rd Corps, Army of Tennessee (July 1864-April 1865)

**Battles:**  Corinth (October 3-4, 1862)

Vicksburg Campaign (May-July 1863)

Champion Hill (May 16, 1863)

Jackson Siege (July 1863)

Meridian Campaign (February-March 1864)

Atlanta Campaign (May-September 1864)

New Hope Church (May 25-June 4, 1864)

Peach Tree Creek (July 20, 1864)

Ezra Church (July 28, 1864)

Atlanta Siege (July-September 1864)

Jonesboro (August 31-September 1, 1864)
Franklin (November 30, 1864)
Nashville (December 15-16, 1864)
Carolinas Campaign (February-April 1865)
Bentonville (March 19-21, 1865)

## 197. MISSISSIPPI 34TH INFANTRY REGIMENT

*Organization:* Organized as the 37th Infantry Regiment ca. April 19, 1862. Redesignated as the 34th Infantry Regiment on March 5, 1863. Field consolidation with the 29th and 30th Infantry Regiments from December 1863 to May 1864. Field consolidation with the 24th and 27th Infantry Regiments in late 1864. Field consolidation with the 24th Infantry Regiment from December 1864 to April 9, 1865. Additional field consolidation with the 27th Infantry Regiment in early 1865. Consolidated with the 24th, 27th, 29th, and 30th Infantry Regiments and designated as the 24th Infantry Regiment. Consolidated at Smithfield, North Carolina on April 9, 1865.

*First Commander:* Samuel Benton (Colonel)

*Field Officers:* Thomas A. Falconer (Major)

Armistead T. Mason (Major)

William G. Pegram (Major)

Hugh A. Reynolds (Major)

Daniel B. Wright (Lieutenant Colonel)

*Assignments:* Walker's Brigade, Ruggles' Division, 2nd Corps, Army of the Mississippi, Department #2 (May 1862)

Anderson's Brigade, Army of the Mississippi, Department #2 (May-June 1862)

Anderson's Brigade, 2nd Corps, Army of the Mississippi, Department #2 (June-July 1862)

Anderson's Brigade, Jones' Division, Army of the Mississippi, Department #2 (July 1862)

T. M. Jones' Brigade, Jones'-Anderson's Division, Left Wing, Army of the Mississippi, Department #2 (October-November 1862)

T. M. Jones' Brigade, Anderson's Division, 1st Corps, Army of Tennessee (November-December 1862)

Anderson's-Walthall's Brigade, Withers'-Hindman's Division, 1st Corps, Army of Tennessee (December 1862-September 1863)

Walthall's Brigade, Liddell's Division, Reserve Corps, Army of Tennessee (September 1863)

Walthall's Brigade, Cheatham's Division, 1st Corps, Army of Tennessee (September 1863-February 1864)

Walthall's-Brantley's Brigade, Hindman's-Anderson's-Johnson's-D. H. Hill's Division, 2nd Corps, Army of Tennessee (February 1864-April 1865)

**Battles:**   Corinth Campaign (April-June 1862)
Farmington (May 9, 1862)
Perryville (October 8, 1862)
Murfreesboro (December 31, 1862-January 3, 1863)
Tullahoma Campaign (June 1863)
Chickamauga (September 19-20, 1863)
Chattanooga Siege (September-November 1863)
Chattanooga (November 23-25, 1863)
Atlanta Campaign (May-September 1864)
Resaca (May 14-15, 1864)
New Hope Church (May 25-June 4, 1864)
Ezra Church (July 28, 1864)
Atlanta Siege (July-September 1864)
Franklin (November 30, 1864)
Nashville (December 15-16, 1864)
Carolinas Campaign (February-April 1865)

## 198.   MISSISSIPPI 35TH INFANTRY REGIMENT

**Organization:**   Organized in the spring of 1862.   Regiment surrendered at Vicksburg, Warren County, Mississippi on July 4, 1863.   Paroled at Vicksburg, Warren County, Mississippi in July 1863.   Declared exchanged on September 12, 1863.   Surrendered by Lieutenant Richard Taylor, commanding the Department of Alabama, Mississippi, and East Louisiana, at Citronelle, Alabama on May 4, 1865.

**First Commander:**   William T.S. Barry (Colonel)

**Field Officers:**   Thomas F. Holmes (Major)
Charles R. Jordan (Lieutenant Colonel)
Reuben H. Shotwell (Lieutenant Colonel)
Oliver C. Watson (Major)

**Assignments:**   Maury's-Moore's Brigade, Jones'-Maury's Division, Army of the West, Department #2 (June-October 1862)
Moore's Brigade, Maury's Division, Price's Corps, Army of West Tennessee, Department of Mississippi and East Louisiana (October-December 1862)
Moore's Brigade, Lee's-Maury's Provisional Division, 2nd Military District, Department of Mississippi and East Louisiana (December 1862-January 1863)
Moore's Brigade, Maury's Division, 2nd Military District, Department of Mississippi and East Louisiana (January-April 1863)
Moore's Brigade, Maury's-Forney's Division, Department of Mississippi and East Louisiana (April-July 1863)

Baldwin's Brigade, Walker's Division, 1st Corps, Army of Tennessee (December 1863-January 1864)

Baldwin's Brigade, Department of the Gulf (January-February 1864)

Baldwin's [old]-Sears' Brigade, Department of Alabama, Mississippi, and East Louisiana (March-May 1864)

Sears' Brigade, Army of Mississippi (May 1864)

Sears' Brigade, French's Division, Army of Mississippi (May-July 1864)

Sears' Brigade, French's Division, 3rd Corps, Army of Tennessee (July 1864-January 1865)

Sears' Brigade, French's Division, District of the Gulf, Department of Alabama, Mississippi, and East Louisiana (January-April 1865)

Sears' Brigade, French's Division, Department of Alabama, Mississippi, and East Louisiana (April-May 1865)

**Battles:**  Corinth (October 3-4, 1862)

Chickasaw Bayou (December 27-29, 1862)

Vicksburg Campaign (May-July 1863)

Vicksburg Siege (May-July 1863)

Atlanta Campaign (May-September 1864)

Cassville (May 19-22, 1864)

New Hope Church (May 25-June 4, 1864)

Lattimer's Mills (June 20, 1864)

Smyrna Campground (July 4, 1864)

Chattahoochee River (July 5-17, 1864)

Peach Tree Creek (July 20, 1864)

Atlanta (July 22, 1864)

Ezra Church (July 28, 1864)

Atlanta Siege (July-September 1864)

Jonesboro (August 31-September 1, 1864)

Lovejoy's Station (September 2-5, 1864)

Allatoona (October 5, 1864)

Franklin (November 30, 1864)

Nashville (December 15-16, 1864)

Mobile (March 17-April 12, 1865)

## 199.  MISSISSIPPI 36TH INFANTRY REGIMENT

*Organization:*  Organized in early 1862. Regiment surrendered at Vicksburg, Warren County, Mississippi on July 4, 1863. Paroled at Vicksburg, Warren County, Mississippi in July 1863. Declared exchanged on September 12, 1863. Surrendered by Lieutenant Richard Taylor, commanding the Department of Alabama, Mississippi, and East Louisiana, at Citronelle, Alabama on May 4, 1865.

*First Commander:*    Drury J. Brown (Colonel)
*Field Officers:*    Edward Brown (Lieutenant Colonel)
S. G. Harper (Lieutenant Colonel)
Charles P. Partin (Major)
William W. Witherspoon (Major)
Alexander Yates (Major)
**Assignments:**    Chalmers' Brigade, Withers' Division, 2nd Corps, Army of the Mississippi, Department #2 (April 1862)
Anderson's Brigade, Ruggles' Division, 2nd Corps, Army of the Mississippi, Department #2 (May 1862)
Chalmers' Brigade, Withers' Division, 2nd Corps, Army of the Mississippi, Department #2 (May 1862)
Martin's Brigade, Little's-Hébert's Division, Price's Corps, Army of West Tennessee, Department #2 (September-October 1862)
Martin's Brigade, Hébert's-Maury's Division, Price's Corps, Army of West Tennessee, Department of Mississippi and East Louisiana (October 1862)
Hébert's Brigade, Maury's Division, 2nd Military District, Department of Mississippi and East Louisiana (December 1862-January 1863)
Hébert's Brigade, Maury's Division, 2nd Military District, Department of Mississippi and East Louisiana (January-April 1863)
Hébert's Brigade, Maury's-Forney's Division, Department of Mississippi and East Louisiana (April-July 1863)
Mackall's Brigade, Department of the Gulf (February 1864)
Baldwin's [old]-Sears' Brigade, Department of Alabama, Mississippi, and East Louisiana (March-May 1864)
Sears' Brigade, Army of Mississippi (May 1864)
Sears' Brigade, French's Division, Army of Mississippi (May-July 1864)
Sears' Brigade, French's Division, 3rd Corps, Army of Tennessee (July 1864-January 1865)
Sears' Brigade, French's Division, District of the Gulf, Department of Alabama, Mississippi, and East Louisiana (January-April 1865)
Sears' Brigade, French's Division, Department of Alabama, Mississippi, and East Louisiana (April-May 1865)
**Battles:**    Corinth Campaign (April-June 1862)
Farmington (May 1862)
Iuka (September 19, 1862)
Corinth (October 3-4, 1862)
Vicksburg Campaign (May-July 1863)
Vicksburg Siege (May-July 1863)
Atlanta Campaign (May-September 1864)
Cassville (May 19-22, 1864)

New Hope Church (May 25-June 4, 1864)
Lattimer's Mills (June 20, 1864)
Kennesaw Mountain (June 27, 1864)
Smyrna Campground (July 4, 1864)
Chattahoochee River (July 5-17, 1864)
Peach Tree Creek (July 20, 1864)
Atlanta (July 22, 1864)
Ezra Church (July 28, 1864)
Atlanta Siege (July-September 1864)
Jonesboro (August 31-September 1, 1864)
Lovejoy's Station (September 2-5, 1864)
Allatoona (October 5, 1864)
Franklin (November 30, 1864)
Nashville (December 15-16, 1864)
Mobile (March 17-April 12, 1865)

## 200. MISSISSIPPI 37TH INFANTRY REGIMENT

*Organization:* Organized in mid-1862. Regiment surrendered at Vicksburg, Warren County, Mississippi on July 4, 1863. Paroled at Vicksburg, Warren County, Mississippi in July 1863. Declared exchanged on September 12, 1863. Surrendered by General Joseph E. Johnston at Durham Station, Orange County, North Carolina on April 26, 1865.

*First Commander:* Robert McLain (Colonel)

*Field Officers:* Q. C. Heidelberg (Major)

Orlando S. Holland (Lieutenant Colonel, Colonel)

John McGee (Major)

William S. Patton (Lieutenant Colonel)

Samuel H. Terral (Major, Lieutenant Colonel)

William W. Wier (Major, Lieutenant Colonel)

*Assignments:* Martin's Brigade, Little's-Hébert's Division, Price's Corps, Army of West Tennessee, Department #2 (September-October 1862)

Martin's Brigade, Hébert's-Maury's Division, Price's Corps, Army of West Tennessee, Department of Mississippi and East Louisiana (October 1862)

Hébert's Brigade, Maury's Division, 2nd Military District, Department of Mississippi and East Louisiana (December 1862-January 1863)

Hébert's Brigade, Maury's Division, 2nd Military District, Department of Mississippi and East Louisiana (January-April 1863)

Hébert's Brigade, Maury's-Forney's Division, Department of Mississippi and East Louisiana (April-July 1863)

Mackall's Brigade, Department of the Gulf (February 1864)

Cantey's Brigade, Cantey's-Walthall's Division, Army of Mississippi (June-July 1864)

Cantey's-Shelley's Brigade, Walthall's Division, 3rd Corps, Army of Tennessee (July-December 1864)

Featherston's Brigade, Loring's Division, 3rd Corps, Army of Tennessee (April 1865)

**Battles:**  Iuka (September 19, 1862)
Corinth Campaign (April-June 1862)
Farmington (May 1862)
Iuka (September 19, 1862)
Corinth (October 3-4, 1862)
Vicksburg Campaign (May-July 1863)
Vicksburg Siege (May-July 1863)
Atlanta Campaign (May-September 1864)
Resaca (May 9, 1864)
Resaca (May 14-15, 1864)
Peach Tree Creek (July 20, 1864)
Ezra Church (July 28, 1864)
Atlanta Siege (July-September 1864)
Jonesboro (August 31-September 1, 1864)
Franklin (November 30, 1864)
Nashville (December 15-16, 1864)
Carolinas Campaign (February-April 1865)
**Further Reading:**  Banks, R. W., *The Battle of Franklin, Tennessee, November 30, 1864.*

## 201.  MISSISSIPPI 37TH (BENTON'S) INFANTRY REGIMENT

*See:* MISSISSIPPI 34TH INFANTRY REGIMENT
**First Commander:**  Fleming W. Adams (Colonel)

## 202.  MISSISSIPPI 38TH INFANTRY REGIMENT

**Also Known As:**  Mississippi 38th Mounted Infantry Regiment
**Organization:**  Organized in mid-1862.  Regiment surrendered at Vicksburg, Warren County, Mississippi on July 4, 1863.  Paroled at Vicksburg, Warren County, Mississippi in July 1863.  Declared exchanged on September 12, 1863. Mounted in early 1864.  Surrendered by Lieutenant Richard Taylor, commanding the Department of Alabama, Mississippi, and East Louisiana, at Citronelle, Alabama on May 4, 1865.
**Field Officers:**  Preston Brent (Lieutenant Colonel, Colonel)
Franklin W. Foxworth (Major)
Walter L. Keirn (Major, Lieutenant Colonel)

Robert C. McCay (Major)

**Assignments:** Martin's Brigade, Little's-Hébert's Division, Price's Corps, Army of West Tennessee, Department #2 (September-October 1862)

Martin's Brigade, Hébert's-Maury's Division, Price's Corps, Army of West Tennessee, Department of Mississippi and East Louisiana (October 1862)

Hébert's Brigade, Maury's Division, 2nd Corps, Army of North Mississippi, Department of Mississippi and East Louisiana (December 1862-January 1863)

Hébert's Brigade, Maury's Division, 2nd Military District, Department of Mississippi and East Louisiana (January-April 1863)

Hébert's Brigade, Maury's-Forney's Division, Department of Mississippi and East Louisiana (April-July 1863)

District of Southwestern Mississippi and East Louisiana, Department of Alabama, Mississippi, and East Louisiana [Company D] (February-May 1864)

Scott's Brigade, Adams' Cavalry Division, Department of Alabama, Mississippi, and East Louisiana [Company D] (May-June 1864)

Mabry's Brigade, W. Adams' Cavalry Division, Department of Alabama, Mississippi, and East Louisiana (June-August 1864)

Mabry's Brigade, District North of Homochitto, Department of Alabama, Mississippi, and East Louisiana (August-October 1864)

Mabry's Brigade, Northern Sub-district, District of Mississippi and East Louisiana, Department of Alabama, Mississippi, and East Louisiana (October 1864-February 1865)

Mabry's Brigade, [Sub-]District of Southern Mississippi and East Louisiana, District of Mississippi and East Louisiana, Department of Alabama, Mississippi, and East Louisiana (February 1865)

Adams' Brigade, Chalmers' Division, Forrest's Cavalry Corps, Department of Alabama, Mississippi, and East Louisiana (February-May 1865)

**Battles:** Iuka (September 19, 1862)

Corinth (October 3-4, 1862)

Vicksburg Campaign (May-July 1863)

Vicksburg Siege (May-July 1863)

A.J. Smith's 2nd Mississippi Invasion (August 1864)

Tupelo (July 14, 1864)

Concord Church (December 1, 1864)

Wilson's Raid (March-April 1865)

## 203. MISSISSIPPI 39TH INFANTRY REGIMENT

**Organization:** Organized in early 1862. Field consolidation with the 1st Infantry Regiment in January 1863. Surrendered at Port Hudson, Louisiana on July 8, 1863. Paroled in July 1863. Surrendered by Lieutenant Richard Taylor, commanding the Department of Alabama, Mississippi, and East Louisiana, at Citronelle, Alabama on May 4, 1865.

**First Commander:** William B. Shelby (Colonel)

**Field Officers:** R. J. Durr (Major)

William E. Ross (Lieutenant Colonel)

W. Monroe Quin (Major)

**Assignments:** Grenada, Mississippi, Department #2 (June 1862)

3rd Sub-district, District of the Mississippi, Department #2 (June-August 1862)

Allen's Brigade, Ruggles' Division, Breckinridge's Command, District of the Mississippi, Department #2 [Company I] (August 1862)

Villepique's Brigade, Lovell's Division, Army of West Tennessee, Department of Mississippi and East Louisiana (October 1862)

Beall's Brigade, 3rd Military District, Department of Mississippi and East Louisiana (October 1862-July 1863)

Baldwin's (old)-Sears' Brigade, Department of Alabama, Mississippi, and East Louisiana (March-May 1864)

Sears' Brigade, Army of Mississippi (May 1864)

Sears' Brigade, French's Division, Army of Mississippi (May-July 1864)

Sears' Brigade, French's Division, 3rd Corps, Army of Tennessee (July 1864-January 1865)

Sears' Brigade, French's Division, District of the Gulf, Department of Alabama, Mississippi, and East Louisiana (January-April 1865)

Sears' Brigade, French's Division, Department of Alabama, Mississippi, and East Louisiana (April-May 1865)

**Battles:** Vicksburg Bombardments [Company I] (May 18-July 27, 1862)

Baton Rouge [Company I] (August 5, 1862)

Corinth (October 3-4, 1862)

Port Hudson Siege (May-July 1863)

Atlanta Campaign (May-September 1864)

Cassville (May 19-22, 1864)

New Hope Church (May 25-June 4, 1864)

Lattimer's Mills (June 20, 1864)

Kennesaw Mountain (June 27, 1864)

Smyrna Campground (July 4, 1864)

Chattahoochee River (July 5-17, 1864)

Peach Tree Creek (July 20, 1864)

Atlanta (July 22, 1864)

Ezra Church (July 28, 1864)

Atlanta Siege (July-September 1864)

Jonesboro (August 31-September 1, 1864)

Lovejoy's Station (September 2-5, 1864)

Allatoona (October 5, 1864)
Franklin (November 30, 1864)
Nashville (December 15-16, 1864)
Mobile (March 17-April 12, 1865)

## 204. MISSISSIPPI 40TH INFANTRY REGIMENT

*Organization:* Organized in mid-1862. Regiment surrendered at Vicksburg, Warren County, Mississippi on July 4, 1863. Paroled at Vicksburg, Warren County, Mississippi in July 1863. Declared exchanged on September 12, 1863. Consolidated with the 3rd and 31st Infantry Regiments and designated as the 3rd Infantry Regiment Consolidated at Smithfield, North Carolina on April 9, 1865.

*First Commander:* W. Bruce Colbert (Colonel)

*Field Officers:* Josiah A. P. Campbell (Lieutenant Colonel)
James R. Childress (Lieutenant Colonel)
William McD. Gibbons (Major)
Enoch McDonald (Major)
George P. Wallace (Lieutenant Colonel, Colonel)

*Assignments:* Hébert's Brigade, Little's-Hébert's Division, Price's Corps, Army of West Tennessee, Department #2 (September-October 1862)
Hébert's Brigade, Hébert's Division, Price's Corps, Army of West Tennessee, Department of Mississippi and East Louisiana (October 1862)
Moore's Brigade, Maury's Division, Price's Corps, Army of West Tennessee, Department of Mississippi and East Louisiana (October 1862-January 1863)
Moore's Brigade, Maury's Division, 2nd Military District, Department of Mississippi and East Louisiana (January-April 1863)
Moore's Brigade, Maury's-Forney's Division, Department of Mississippi and East Louisiana (April-July 1863)
Baldwin's Brigade, Walker's Division, 1st Corps, Army of Tennessee (December 1863-January 1864)
Baldwin's Brigade, Department of the Gulf (January-February 1864)
Featherston's Brigade, Loring's Division, Department of Alabama, Mississippi, and East Louisiana (March-May 1864)
Featherston's Brigade, Loring's Division, Army of Mississippi (May-July 1864)
Featherston's Brigade, Loring's Division, 3rd Corps, Army of Tennessee (July 1864-April 1865)

*Battles:* Iuka (September 19, 1862)
Corinth (October 3-4, 1862)
Vicksburg Campaign (May-July 1863)
Vicksburg Siege (May-July 1863)
Atlanta Campaign (May-September 1864)

New Hope Church (May 25-June 4, 1864)
Peach Tree Creek (July 20, 1864)
Ezra Church (July 28, 1864)
Atlanta Siege (July-September 1864)
Jonesboro (August 31-September 1, 1864)
Franklin (November 30, 1864)
Nashville (December 15-16, 1864)
Carolinas Campaign (February-April 1865)

## 205. MISSISSIPPI 41ST INFANTRY REGIMENT

*Organization:*  Organized with 11 companies ca. May 8, 1862. Consolidated with the 7th, 9th, 10th, and 44th Infantry Regiments and the 9th Sharpshooters Battalion and designated as the 9th Infantry Regiment. Consolidated at Smithfield, North Carolina on April 9, 1865.
*First Commander:*  William F. Tucker (Colonel)
*Field Officers:*  Lewis Ball (Major, Colonel)
William C. Hearn (Lieutenant Colonel)
Lafayette Hodges (Major, Lieutenant Colonel)
J. Byrd Williams (Major, Lieutenant Colonel, Colonel)
*Assignments:*  Anderson's Brigade, 2nd Corps, Army of the Mississippi, Department #2 (June-July 1862)
Anderson's Brigade, Jones' Division, Army of the Mississippi, Department #2 (July-August 1862)
Brown's Brigade, Jones'-Anderson's Division, Left Wing, Army of the Mississippi, Department #2 (August-November 1862)
Brown's Brigade, Anderson's Division, 2nd Corps, Army of Tennessee (November-December 1862)
Chalmers'-Anderson's Brigade, Withers'-Hindman's Division, 1st Corps, Army of Tennessee (December 1862-November 1863)
Anderson's-Tucker's-Sharp's Brigade, Hindman's-Anderson's-Johnson's-D. H. Hill's Division, 2nd Corps, Army of Tennessee (November 1863-April 1865)
*Battles:*  Corinth [skirmish] (May 21, 1862)
Perryville (October 8, 1862)
Murfreesboro (December 31, 1862-January 3, 1863)
Rover (February 13, 1863)
Unionville [skirmish] (March 4, 1863)
Tullahoma Campaign (June 1863)
Chickamauga (September 19-20, 1863)
Chattanooga Siege (September-November 1863)
Chattanooga (November 23-25, 1863)
Atlanta Campaign (May-September 1864)

Resaca (May 14-15, 1864)
New Hope Church (May 25-June 4, 1864)
Marietta (June 22, 1864)
Kennesaw Mountain (June 27, 1864)
Atlanta (July 22, 1864)
Atlanta Siege (July-September 1864)
Jonesboro (August 31-September 1, 1864)
Franklin (November 30, 1864)
Nashville (December 15-16, 1864)
Carolinas Campaign (February-April 1865)

## 206.  MISSISSIPPI 42ND INFANTRY REGIMENT

*Organization:*  Organized on May 14, 1862.  Surrendered at Appomattox Court House, Virginia on April 9, 1865.
*First Commander:*  Hugh R. Miller (Colonel)
*Field Officers:*  William A. Feeney (Major, Colonel)
Robert W. Locke (Major)
Hillary Moseley (Lieutenant Colonel)
Andrew M. Nelson (Lieutenant Colonel, Colonel)
*Assignments:*  Grenada, Mississippi, Department #2 (June 1862)
Department of Henrico (July-September 1862)
Unattached, Department of North Carolina and Southern Virginia (September-November 1862)
Davis' Brigade, Unattached, Department of North Carolina and Southern Virginia (December 1862)
Davis' Brigade, French's Command, Department of North Carolina and Southern Virginia (December 1862-February 1863)
Davis' Brigade, Department of Southern Virginia (May 1863)
Davis' Brigade, Department of North Carolina (May 1863)
Davis' Brigade, Heth's Division, 3rd Corps, Army of Northern Virginia (May 1863-April 1865)
*Battles:*  Gettysburg (July 1-3, 1863)
Falling Waters (July 14, 1863)
Bristoe Campaign (October 1863)
Mine Run Campaign (November-December 1863)
The Wilderness (May 5-6, 1864)
Spotsylvania Court House (May 8-21, 1864)
North Anna (May 23-26, 1864)
Cold Harbor (June 1-3, 1864)
Petersburg Siege (June 1864-April 1865)
Weldon Railroad (August 18-22, 1864)

Hatcher's Run (February 5-7, 1865)
Appomattox Court House (April 9, 1865)

## 207. MISSISSIPPI 42ND MOUNTED INFANTRY REGIMENT
*See:* MISSISSIPPI 2ND CAVALRY REGIMENT

## 208. MISSISSIPPI 43RD INFANTRY REGIMENT

**Organization:** Organized in mid-1862. Regiment surrendered at Vicksburg, Warren County, Mississippi on July 4, 1863. Paroled at Vicksburg, Warren County, Mississippi in July 1863. Declared exchanged on September 12, 1863. Consolidated with the 14th Infantry Regiment and part of the 5th Infantry Regiment and designated as the 14th Infantry Regiment Consolidated at Smithfield, North Carolina on April 9, 1865.

**First Commander:** William H. Moore (Colonel)

**Field Officers:** James O. Banks (Major, Lieutenant Colonel)
Richard Harrison (Major, Lieutenant Colonel, Colonel)
Richard W. Leigh (Lieutenant Colonel)
Columbus Sykes (Major, Lieutenant Colonel)

**Assignments:** Green's Brigade, Little's-Hébert's Division, Price's Corps, Army of West Tennessee, Department #2 (September-October 1862)

Green's Brigade, Hébert's Division, Price's Corps, Army of West Tennessee, Department of Mississippi and East Louisiana (October 1862)

Hébert's Brigade, Maury's Division, Price's Corps, Army of West Tennessee, Department of Mississippi and East Louisiana (October 1862)

Hébert's Brigade, Maury's Division, Price's Corps, Army of North Mississippi, Department of Mississippi and East Louisiana (December 1862-January 1863)

Hébert's Brigade, Maury's Division, 2nd Military District, Department of Mississippi and East Louisiana (January-April 1863)

Hébert's Brigade, Maury's-Forney's Division, Department of Mississippi and East Louisiana (April-July 1863)

Mackall's Brigade, Department of the Gulf (February-March 1864)

Featherston's Brigade, Loring's Division, Department of Alabama, Mississippi, and East Louisiana (April-May 1864)

Adams' Brigade, Loring's Division, Department of Alabama, Mississippi, and East Louisiana (May 1864)

Adams' Brigade, Loring's Division, Army of Mississippi (May-July 1864)

Adams' Brigade, Loring's Division, 3rd Corps, Army of Tennessee (July 1864-April 1865)

**Battles:** Iuka (September 19, 1862)
Corinth (October 3-4, 1862)

Vicksburg Campaign (May-July 1863)
Vicksburg Siege (May-July 1863)
Atlanta Campaign (May-September 1864)
New Hope Church (May 25-June 4, 1864)
Peach Tree Creek (July 20, 1864)
Atlanta (July 22, 1864)
Ezra Church (July 28, 1864)
Atlanta Siege (July-September 1864)
Jonesboro (August 31-September 1, 1864)
Franklin (November 30, 1864)
Nashville (December 15-16, 1864)
Carolinas Campaign (February-April 1865)

## 209. MISSISSIPPI 44TH INFANTRY REGIMENT

*Nickname:* Blythe's Infantry Regiment

*Organization:* Organized by the change of designation of Blythe's Infantry Regiment in the spring of 1862. Field consolidation with the 10th Infantry Regiment at various times from November 1863 to April 9, 1865. Additional field consolidation with the 9th Sharpshooters Battalion from November 1864 to April 9, 1865. Consolidated with the 7th, 9th, 10th, and 41st Infantry Regiments and the 9th Sharpshooters Battalion and designated as the 9th Infantry Regiment Consolidated at Smithfield, North Carolina on April 9, 1865.

*First Commander:* Jacob H. Sharp (Colonel)

*Field Officers:* R. G. Kelsey (Major, Lieutenant Colonel)
James Moore (Major)
William T. Nesbit (Lieutenant Colonel)
William H. Sims (Lieutenant Colonel)
John C. Thompson (Major)

*Assignments:* Trapier's Brigade, Withers' Division, 2nd Corps, Army of the Mississippi, Department #2 (April-May 1862)
Chalmers' Brigade, Withers' Division, 2nd Corps, Army of the Mississippi, Department #2 (June 1862)
Chalmers' Brigade, Reserve Corps, Army of the Mississippi, Department #2 (June-July 1862)
Chalmers' Brigade, Withers' Division, Army of the Mississippi, Department #2 (July-August 1862)
Chalmers' Brigade, Withers' Division, Right Wing, Army of the Mississippi, Department #2 (August-October 1862)
Jackson's Brigade, Withers' Division, Right Wing, Army of the Mississippi, Department #2 (November 1862)

Jackson's Brigade, Withers' Division, 1st Corps, Army of Tennessee (November 1862)

Chalmers'-White's-Anderson's Brigade, Withers'-Hindman's Division (November 1862-December 1863)

Anderson's-Tucker's-Sharp's Brigade, Hindman's-Anderson's-Johnson's-D. H. Hill's Division, 2nd Corps, Army of Tennessee (December 1863-April 1865)

**Battles:**  Corinth Campaign (April-June 1862)

Munfordville (September 17, 1862)

Murfreesboro (December 31, 1862-January 3, 1863)

Rover (February 13, 1863)

Tullahoma Campaign (June 1863)

Chickamauga (September 19-20, 1863)

Chattanooga Siege (September-November 1863)

Chattanooga (November 23-25, 1863)

Atlanta Campaign (May-September 1864)

Resaca (May 14-15, 1864)

New Hope Church (May 25-June 4, 1864)

Atlanta Siege (July-September 1864)

Franklin (November 30, 1864)

Nashville (December 15-16, 1864)

Carolinas Campaign (February-April 1865)

## 210.  MISSISSIPPI 45TH INFANTRY REGIMENT

*Also Known As:*  33rd Infantry Regiment

*Organization:*  Organized by the increase of the 3rd (Hardcastle's) Infantry Battalion to a regiment and designated as the 33rd (Hardcastle's) Infantry Regiment in April 1862.  Designated as the 45th Infantry Regiment in 1863. Field consolidation with the 32nd Infantry Regiment in 1863 and 1864. Reduced to a battalion and designated as the 3rd (Williams') Infantry Battalion on July 24, 1864.

*First Commander:*  Aaron R. Hardcastle (Colonel)

*Field Officers:*  Richard Charlton (Lieutenant Colonel)

Theodore A. Jones (Major)

Charles P. Neilson (Lieutenant Colonel)

Elisha F. Nunn (Major)

*Assignments:*  Wood's Brigade, 3rd Corps, Army of the Mississippi, Department #2 (April-July 1862)

Wood's Brigade, Hardee's-Buckner's Division, Army of the Mississippi, Department #2 (July-August 1862)

Wood's Brigade, Buckner's Division, Left Wing, Army of the Mississippi, Department #2 (August-November 1862)

Wood's-Lowrey's Brigade, Buckner's-Cleburne's Division, 2nd Corps, Army of Tennessee (November 1862-November 1863)

Lowrey's Brigade, Cleburne's Division, 1st Corps, Army of Tennessee (November 1863-July 1864)

**Battles:** Corinth Campaign (April-June 1862)

Perryville (October 8, 1862)

Murfreesboro (December 31, 1862-January 3, 1863)

Tullahoma Campaign (June 1863)

Chickamauga (September 19-20, 1863)

Chattanooga Siege (September-November 1863)

Chattanooga (November 23-25, 1863)

Atlanta Campaign (May-September 1864)

New Hope Church (May 25-June 4, 1864)

Kennesaw Mountain (June 27, 1864)

Atlanta (July 22, 1864)

## 211. MISSISSIPPI 46TH INFANTRY REGIMENT

*Also Known As:* 49th Infantry Regiment

*Organization:* Organized in late 1862. Regiment surrendered at Vicksburg, Warren County, Mississippi on July 4, 1863. Paroled at Vicksburg, Warren County, Mississippi in July 1863. Declared exchanged on September 12, 1863. Surrendered by Lieutenant Richard Taylor, commanding the Department of Alabama, Mississippi, and East Louisiana, at Citronelle, Alabama on May 4, 1865.

*First Commander:* John W. Balfour (Colonel)

*Field Officers:* William H. Clark (Major, Lieutenant Colonel, Colonel)

William K. Easterling (Lieutenant Colonel)

Turpin D. Magee (Major)

Constantine Rae (Major)

Claudius W. Sears (Colonel)

*Assignments:* Thomas' Brigade, Lee's-Maury's Division, 2nd Military District, Department of Mississippi and East Louisiana (December 1862-January 1863)

Lee's-Baldwin's Brigade, Smith's Division, 2nd Military District, Department of Mississippi and East Louisiana (January-April 1863)

Baldwin's Brigade, Smith's Division, Department of Mississippi and East Louisiana (April-July 1863)

Baldwin's Brigade, Walker's Division, 1st Corps, Army of Tennessee (December 1863-January 1864)

Baldwin's Brigade, Department of the Gulf (January-February 1864)

Baldwin's (old)-Sears' Brigade, Department of Alabama, Mississippi, and East
    Louisiana (March-May 1864)
Sears' Brigade, Army of Mississippi (May 1864)
Sears' Brigade, French's Division, Army of Mississippi (May-July 1864)
Sears' Brigade, French's Division, 3rd Corps, Army of Tennessee (July 1864-
    January 1865)
Sears' Brigade, French's Division, District of the Gulf, Department of Alabama,
    Mississippi, and East Louisiana (January-April 1865)
Sears' Brigade, French's Division, Department of Alabama, Mississippi, and
    East Louisiana (April-May 1865)
**Battles:** Chickasaw Bayou (December 27-29, 1862)
Vicksburg Passage (April 16, 1863)
Port Gibson (May 1, 1863)
Vicksburg Campaign (May-July 1863)
Vicksburg Siege (May-July 1863)
Atlanta Campaign (May-September 1864)
Cassville (May 19-22, 1864)
New Hope Church (May 25-June 4, 1864)
Lattimer's Mills (June 20, 1864)
Kennesaw Mountain (June 27, 1864)
Smyrna Campground (July 4, 1864)
Chattahoochee River (July 5-17, 1864)
Peach Tree Creek (July 20, 1864)
Atlanta (July 22, 1864)
Ezra Church (July 28, 1864)
Atlanta Siege (July-September 1864)
Jonesboro (August 31-September 1, 1864)
Lovejoy's Station (September 2-5, 1864)
Allatoona (October 5, 1864)
Franklin (November 30, 1864)
Nashville (December 15-16, 1864)
Mobile (March 17-April 12, 1865)

## 212. MISSISSIPPI 48TH INFANTRY REGIMENT

**Organization:** Organized by the increase of the 2nd Infantry Battalion to a
regiment on January 17, 1863. Surrendered at Appomattox Court House,
Virginia on April 9, 1865.
**First Commander:** Joseph M. Jayne (Colonel)
**Field Officers:** Levi C. Lee (Major)
Thomas B. Manlove (Lieutenant Colonel)

*Assignments:*  Featherston's-Posey's Brigade, R. H. Anderson's Division, 1st
  Corps, Army of Northern Virginia (January-May 1863)
Posey's-Harris' Brigade, Anderson's-Mahone's Division, 3rd Corps, Army of
  Northern Virginia (May 1863-April 1865)
*Battles:*  Chancellorsville (May 1-4, 1863)
Gettysburg (July 1-3, 1863)
Bristoe Campaign (October 1863)
Mine Run Campaign (November-December 1863)
The Wilderness (May 5-6, 1864)
Spotsylvania Court House (May 8-21, 1864)
North Anna (May 23-26, 1864)
Cold Harbor (June 1-3, 1864)
Petersburg Siege (June 1864-April 1865)
Appomattox Court House (April 9, 1865)

## 213.  MISSISSIPPI 49TH (BALFOUR'S-SEARS'-CLARK'S) INFANTRY REGIMENT

*See:* MISSISSIPPI 46TH INFANTRY REGIMENT

## 214.  MISSISSIPPI BLYTHE'S INFANTRY REGIMENT

*Organization:*  Organized by the increase of the 1st (Blythe's) Infantry Battalion to a regiment in the fall of 1861.  Designation changed to the 44th Infantry Regiment in 1862.
*First Commander:*  Andrew K. Blythe (Colonel)
*Field Officers:*  D. L. Herron (Lieutenant Colonel)
James Moore (Major)
*Assignments:*  1st (Smith's) Brigade, 2nd (Cheatham's) Division, 1st Geographical Division, Department #2 (November 1861-March 1862)
Smith's Brigade, 1st Grand Division, Army of the Mississippi, Department #2
  (March 1862)
Johnson's-Smith's Brigade, Cheatham's Division, 1st Corps, Army of the
  Mississippi, Department #2 (March-April 1862)
Trapier's Brigade, Withers' Division, 2nd Corps, Army of the Mississippi,
  Department #2 (April-May 1862)
*Battles:*  Belmont (November 7, 1861)
Shiloh (April 6-7, 1862)

## 215.  MISSISSIPPI CARUTHERS' INFANTRY BATTALION, SHARPSHOOTERS

*Organization:*  Organized in the fall of 1862.  Apparently disbanded later in the year.

*First Commander:* Camillus K. Caruthers (Acting Major)

*Assignment:* Bowen's Brigade, Lovell's Division, District of the Mississippi, Price's Corps, Army of West Tennessee, Department of Mississippi and East Louisiana (October 1862)

*Battle:* Corinth (October 3-4, 1862)

## 216. MISSISSIPPI GILLENLAND'S INFANTRY BATTALION, STATE TROOPS

*Organization:* Organized in state service. This battalion does not appear in the *Official Records.*

*First Commander:* D. C. Gillenland (Major)

## 217. MISSISSIPPI REA'S INFANTRY BATTALION, SHARPSHOOTERS

*Organization:* This battalion does not appear in the *Official Records.*

*First Commander:* Constantine Rea (Major)

# BIBLIOGRAPHY

Amman, William. *Personnel of the Civil War.* 2 volumes. New York: Thomas Yoseloff, 1961. Provides valuable information on local unit designations, general officers' assignments and organizational data on geographical commands.

Boatner, Mark Mayo III. *The Civil War Dictionary.* New York: David McKay Company, 1959. Provides thumbnail sketches of leaders, battles, campaigns, events and units.

Bowman, John S. *The Civil War Almanac.* New York: Facts On File, 1982. Basically a chronology, it is valuable for its 130 biographical sketches, many of them military personalities.

Daniel, Larry J. *Cannoneers in Gray: The Field Artillery of the Army of Tennessee, 1861–1865.* University, Alabama. University of Alabama Press, 1984. An excellent study of the artillery in the western theater.

Evans, Clement A., ed. *Confederate Military History.* 13 volumes. Atlanta: Confederate Publishing Company, 1899. Each volume of this series primarily provides the histories of one or two states. Each state military account was written by a different participant in the war, and they vary greatly in quality. All accounts, however, include biographies of the generals from their state. The lack of a comprehensive index is the major drawback of this work. Volume XII includes the Mississippi chapter by Colonel Charles E. Hooker.

Freeman, Douglas Southall. *Lee's Lieutenants: A Study in Command.* 3 volumes. New York: Charles Scribner's Sons, 1941–1946. The premier narrative study of the organizational and command structure of the Army of Northern Virginia.

———. *R.E. Lee: A Biography.* 4 volumes. New York: Charles Scribner's Sons, 1934–1935. Also provides organizational information on the Army of Northern Virginia.

Johnson, Robert Underwood, and Buel, Clarence Clough, eds. *Battle and Leaders of the Civil War.* 4 volumes. New York: The Century Company, 1887.

Reprinted 1956. Exceptionally valuable for its tables of organization for major engagements.

Krick, Robert K. *Lee's Colonels: A Biographical Register of the Field Officers of the Army of Northern Virginia*. 2nd edition. Dayton, Ohio: Press of Morningside Bookstore, 1984. Brief but very informative sketches of the 1,965 field-grade officers who at one time or another served with the Army of Northern Virginia but never achieved the the rank of brigadier general. The second edition also includes a listing by name and unit of those field-grade officers who never served with Lee.

Long, E.B. and Barbara. *The Civil War Day By Day: An Almanac 1861–1865*. Garden City, New York: Doubleday, 1971. An excellent chronology of the conflict, with much information on the organizational changes command assignments.

Lonn, Ella. *Foreigners in the Confederacy*. Chapel Hill: University of North Carolina, 1940. Accounts of the foreign-born contribution to the Confederacy.

National Archives, Record Group 109. Microfilm compilation of the service records of every known Confederate soldier, organized by unit. The caption cards and record-of-events cards at the beginning of each unit provide much valuable information on the units' organizational history.

Scharf, J. Thomas. *History of the Confederate States Navy: From Its Organization to the Surrender of Its Last Vessels*. Albany: Joseph McDonough, 1887. A rather disjointed narrative that provides some insight into operations along the Southern coast and on the inland waterways. Unfortunately, it lacks an adequate index.

Sifakis, Stewart. *Who Was Who in the Civil War*. New York: Facts On File, 1988.

———. *Who Was Who in the Confederacy*. New York: Facts On File, 1989. Together both works include biographies of over 1,000 participants who served the South during the Civil War. The military entries include much information on regiments and higher commands.

U.S. Navy Department. *Official Records of the Union and Confederate Navies in the War of the Rebellion*. 31 volumes. Washington: Government Printing Office, 1894–1927. Provides much valuable information on the coastal and riverine operations of the Civil War.

U.S. War Department. *The War of the Rebellion: A Compilation of the Official Records of the Union and Confederate Armies*. 70 volumes in 128 books divided into four series, plus atlas. Washington: Government Printing Office, 1881–1901. While difficult to use, this set provides a gold mine of information. Organized by campaigns in specified geographic regions, the volumes are divided into postaction reports and correspondence. The information contained in the hundreds of organizational tables proved invaluable for my purposes.

Wakelyn, Jon L. *Biographical Dictionary of the Confederacy*. Westport, Conn.: Greenwood Press, 1977. Short biographies of 651 leaders of the Confederacy. However, the selection criteria among the military leaders is somewhat haphazard.

Warner Ezra J. *Generals in Gray: Lives of the Confederate Commanders*. Baton Rouge: Louisiana State University Press, 1959. Sketches of the 425 Southern generals. Good coverage of pre- and postwar careers. The wartime portion of the entries leaves something to be desired.

Wise, Jennings Cropper. *The Long Arm of Lee: The History of the Artillery of the Army of Northern Virginia*. Lynchburg, Virginia: J.P. Bell Co., 1915. Reprinted 1959. An excellent study of Lee's artillery, providing valuable information on batteries and their commanders and organizational assignments.

Wright, Marcus J. *General Officers of the Confederate Army*. New York: Neale Publishing Co., 1911. Long the definitive work on the Confederate command structure, it was superseded by Ezra J. Warner's work.

# PERIODICALS

*Civil War Times Illustrated,* its predecessor *Civil War Times, American History Illustrated* and *Civil War History.* In addition, the *Southern Historical Society Papers* (47 vols., 1876–1930) are a gold mine of information on Confederate units and leaders.

# MISSISSIPPI
# BATTLES

References are to record numbers, not page numbers.

1st Bull Run, Virginia 135, 166 [two companies], 169, 176, 177

2nd Bull Run, Virginia 133, 135, 166, 167, 175, 178

Abbeville 70

Allatoona, Georgia 147, 155, 198, 199, 203, 211

Allen's Farm, Virginia 176, 177, 181

Amite River, Louisiana 47 [Company H]

Antietam, Maryland 109, 133, 135, 166, 167, 169, 175, 176, 177, 178, 181

Appomattox Court House, Virginia 22, 31, 135, 166, 167, 169, 175, 176, 177, 178, 181, 188, 206, 212

Athens, Alabama 32

Atlanta, Georgia 147, 150, 155, 160, 194, 198, 199, 203, 205, 208, 210, 211

Atlanta Campaign, Georgia 9, 17, 19, 28, 37, 39, 43, 47, 59, 65, 75, 77, 78, 91, 127, 129, 140, 142,

147, 150, 154, 155, 156, 160, 161, 162, 165, 170, 173, 180, 182, 184, 185, 189, 191, 192, 193, 194, 196, 197, 198, 199, 200, 203, 204, 205, 208, 209, 210, 211

Atlanta Siege, Georgia 9, 17, 19, 28, 37, 39, 43, 47, 58, 59, 65, 75, 77, 78, 91, 127, 129, 140, 142, 147, 150, 154, 155, 156, 160, 161, 162, 165, 170, 173, 180, 182, 184, 185, 189, 191, 192, 193, 194, 196, 197, 198, 199, 200, 203, 204, 205, 208, 209, 211

Austin 59

Ball's Bluff, Virginia 169 [Company D], 176, 177

*Barataria*, Amite River 47

Baton Rouge, Louisiana 32, 173, 182, 193, 203 [Company I]

Belmont, Missouri 37, 45, 214

Bentonville, North Carolina 75, 76, 140, 150,

160, 173, 180, 182, 184, 196

Berryville, Virginia 176, 177, 181

Bethesda Church, Virginia 188

Big Black River Bridge 94

Biloxi 142

Blackburn's Ford, Virginia 176, 177

Brandy Station, Virginia 109

Brentwood, Tennessee 58

Brice's Crossroads 74, 85

Bristoe Campaign, Virginia 31, 109, 135, 166, 167, 175, 178, 206, 212

Brownsville, Kentucky 43

Bunker Hill, West Virginia 176, 177, 181

Campbellton, Georgia 47, 58, 59, 91

Canton 36, 40

Carolinas Campaign 43, 75, 76, 77, 109, 127, 129, 140, 142, 143, 150, 154, 156, 158, 160, 161, 162, 163, 165, 170, 171, 173, 174, 180, 182, 183,

# MISSISSIPPI NAME INDEX

References are to record numbers, not page numbers.